'Here is a theologically informed and practically based handbook to encourage seekers of God and strengthen Christians in their journey of faith. The challenge and joy of being a disciple is woven into the call of mission and a life shaped by the Eucharist. Written by seasoned practitioners, this is an excellent resource for confirmation groups, general enquirers and people of faith who want to go deeper. The group sessions and leader's guides are superb. The book will confirm faith and energize disciples.'

The Rt Revd Dr Stephen Pickard, Director
Oxford Centre for Ecclesiology and Practical Theology

'For those who think disciple-making began in West London with the "Alpha" course, Being God's People reminds us that catechesis has its roots in the earliest period of the Church's life, and throughout its life, the Church has sought to form disciples after the pattern of Jesus Christ. Structured around the shape of the Eucharist, this course provides for the modern Catholic wings of every Church what Alpha and Emmaus have provided elsewhere for Evangelicals. While obviously written with an Anglican parish in mind, with some adaptation of language, however, it could equally serve a broader ecumenical constituency, especially wherever the Eucharist forms the guiding structure for faith and practice. This course written by Greenwood and Hart is biblical, practical and imaginative, and faithful to the teaching of the Church. Forming individuals and a community around the habitus of the Eucharist is ages old and yet contemporary in its challenge to individualism and consumerism, and I welcome this new resource to the armoury of discipleship-making and community-forming that is always the task of the congregation and its ministers.'

The Revd Dr Paul Goodliff, Head of Ministry
Baptist Union of Great Britain

'A rare combination: a resource with a well-thought-out theology and a lively, creative and open learning structure for small groups. In *Being God's People*, Robin Greenwood and Sue Hart provide us with a rich resource which will be used in parishes for confirmation preparation and, beyond that, for the nurturing of disciples alive to God and the world around them.'

The Revd Dr Roger L. Walton, William Leech Research Fellow
Department of Theology and Religion, Durham University

'The Eucharist is at the heart of the Church's life. Through chapters rich in food for spiritual thought and plans for experiential encounters that engage God's people with one another, Greenwood and Hart take us on a ten-session journey deeply into this core reality of the Christian faith, unlocking its potential in the power of the Spirit to more fully form disciples among those preparing for confirmation and those seeking a richer life of faith. Following the movements that gave shape to the celebration of the Eucharist, this course in discipleship promises to enrich the experience of worship and to enliven the Church in its mission in and for the world.'

Bishop Robert Alan Rimbo, Metropolitan New York Synod
Evangelical Lutheran Church in America

'Being God's People will, I hope, be a valued resource for local churches which take seriously their adult Christian nurture at a time in history when the making of disciples could not be more important. Robin Greenwood's no-nonsense theological linking of the Eucharist to Christian living is paired in each chapter with a section that celebrates and helps groups to take ownership of the material.'

The Rt Revd Robert Paterson, Bishop of Sodor and Man

Robin Greenwood is Vicar of St Mary's, Monkseaton, in Whitley Bay and Canon Emeritus of Chelmsford Cathedral. In 40 years of ordained ministry within the Church of England he has served in parishes, cathedrals and training teams. As a practical theologian, he has resourced conferences in the UK, the USA, Australia and New Zealand. An accomplished author, his works include: *The Ministry Team Handbook* (2000), *Transforming Priesthood* (2002), *Local Ministry* (2006), *Risking Everything* (2006) and *Parish Priests* (2009), all published by SPCK.

Sue Hart has been a Reader at St Mary's, Monkseaton, for more than ten years. She is secretary to the Readers' Board in the Diocese of Newcastle, a member of the Central Readers' Council and is the national consultant for quality in Reader education. As a qualified graphic designer and advertising copywriter, she has worked in art and design education for more than 40 years as a senior manager, lecturer and external consultant and adviser for standards moderation in further and higher education across the country.

Being God's People

*The Confirmation and
Discipleship Handbook*

ROBIN GREENWOOD

and

SUE HART

First published in Great Britain in 2011

Society for Promoting Christian Knowledge
36 Causton Street
London SW1P 4ST
www.spckpublishing.co.uk

British Library Cataloguing-in-Publication Data
A catalogue record for this book is available from the British Library

ISBN: 978–0–281–06361–1
eBook ISBN: 978–0–281–06678–0

Typeset by Caroline Waldron, Wirral, Cheshire
First printed in Great Britain by Ashford Colour Press
Subsequently digitally reprinted in Great Britain

Produced on paper from sustainable forests

For eucharistic communities worldwide,
seeking solidarity with God's work
in the whole of life

Contents

Figures

Foreword

Returning recently to preach at St Mary's, where Robin and Sue both now minister, I was struck by the debt I owe to that community. More than a quarter of a century on from serving as a deaconess, I appreciated much more deeply the nurture the congregation offered, their challenge in the face of new ideas and, with the local community, their willingness to take seriously a 'twenty-something' trying to talk about God.

Of course the clergy with whom I served, as well as laity in formal roles, made highly significant contributions to my learning; but retrospectively I am reminded forcibly why we talk about 'training parishes' as well as 'training incumbents'. The community where we train is as important as the individuals who train us.

At a human and at a divine level there is no surprise in this. We know we cannot 'go it alone'. We know too that we can only be Godlike in community. The Trinity graphically points it out. We act it out each time we gather to celebrate the Eucharist. These are simple truths for the Christian, but in a world where community is fractured and societies and nations struggle, a gift for others. Community as a place of learning, nurture and celebration is desperately needed.

In this context Robin and Sue's handbook offers leaders of all kinds a resource for developing faith and helping people discover or rediscover Christianity. The book is deeply embedded in an understanding of community, God and the Eucharist, owing its own debt to Robin's long-term study of Christian teaching and ministry. It is a practical handbook, in which Sue follows through these elements with a structure that draws out the eucharistic offering of celebration – the fun as well as the profundity. The group work models choice for leaders, care and attention to detail and a way of 'travelling together differently' in discipleship.

These are recipes tried and tested with the local community, so Robin and Sue practise what they preach. I wish it had been around for the twenty-something deaconess to use in Confirmation preparation all those years ago.

The Venerable Sheila Watson
Archdeacon of Canterbury

Preface

We offer this handbook as:

1   A resource to be used and adapted by clergy, Readers and all – ecumenically where possible – who have responsibility for developing faith in local churches, corporate and personal.

2   Ten short chapters by Robin, to be used by anyone leading or participating in a faith-development course. Written especially within an Anglican situation, we hope this material may connect with a wide variety of Christians.

3   Ten learning processes by Sue, opening up the themes of each chapter in conversation, prayer, creativity and hospitality.

For six years, in a modern catholic setting, we have worked together within a wider team on learning processes for the local church community serving the entire neighbourhood. We are proud, at the outset, to own faith in God who, as loving and outward-facing interrelation, is among us and constantly working in the world. This Trinitarian God we worship and serve in community and public life shapes our way of practising Christian community as inherently mutual.

Our understanding of mission, Church, discipleship, human maturity and Eucharist speaks of abundance and blessing, as God's gifts given in community. As faithful witnesses we are called to seek the welfare of every situation in which we are placed, an advance sign of God's final hope for creation.

Inevitably, then, we challenge and offer an alternative to individualistic and adversarial accounts of Christian faith and human solidarity. Our approach, rooted in Scripture and reflection on Christ's presence in all the particulars of life, takes as its background canvas God's work in the world characterized as generous, open and engaged. The baseline for this handbook is the belief that God's people exist as a learning, pilgrim community in which *everyone is a contributor, whatever his or her role*. Figure 1 (overleaf) shows key elements of this.

So this is the viewpoint from which we advocate a eucharistically shaped Mission within the Anglican tradition. We hope that others will be able to find encouragement here too, even though your view may be from a different point. In our own local church community we offer a variety of forms of worship, especially for those who are seeking faith. But we recognize how much we are formed by the radical openness of the Eucharist, and want to commend to others the work of

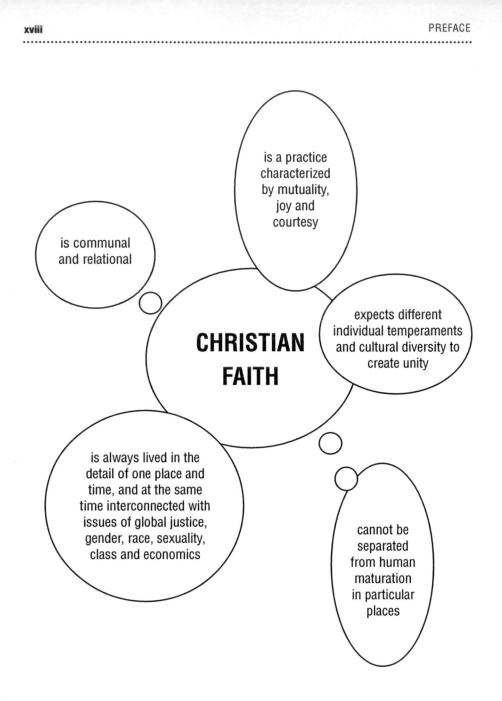

is a practice characterized by mutuality, joy and courtesy

is communal and relational

CHRISTIAN FAITH

expects different individual temperaments and cultural diversity to create unity

is always lived in the detail of one place and time, and at the same time interconnected with issues of global justice, gender, race, sexuality, class and economics

cannot be separated from human maturation in particular places

Figure 1: The faith of a learning pilgrim community

building on the tradition we have received, developing and adapting it in ever new circumstances.

We're not offering here a commentary on the Eucharist itself but discovering in the shape of the eucharistic celebration the entire meaning of Christian discipleship and mission. The eucharistic practice of early churches, as communities of the resurrection in many different locations, was formed long before the first words of the New Testament were written.

As Paul writes in 1 Corinthians, the essential dimensions of the Eucharist are a distillation of all that it means to be a Christian community, serving God's purposes (1 Cor. 11.23–end). The habits formed in the eucharistic celebration take many shapes, through immersion in and constant redevelopment of this tradition handed on to us 'from the Lord' (1 Cor. 11.23).

We invite people in church communities to dare to grow further into intimacy with God and participate in the coming of God's kingdom for the world.

The sessions

These sessions offer practical encouragement to local churches to be creative in deepening the corporate practice of Christian Hope. For some this may be:

- the first chance of this kind ever;
- the time to renew the commitment of Confirmation;
- the journey towards Confirmation;
- the chance to be converted again;
- the gateway to journeys of faith not yet imagined;
- the opportunity to evaluate the life and work of their church.

Robin's particular contribution lies in the brief chapters, while Sue's mainly lies in helping leaders and group members to reflect on them, as a stimulus for their own growth in faith. Sue writes: 'These sessions are for willing workers who struggle a bit with making what is in their hearts a reality.'

Churches and individuals could use this handbook in several ways. First, in a group, alone or as a church, depending on numbers, you could simply read and reflect on the chapters, which offer a rapid framework of Christian community belief and practice. Second, clergy, Readers or lay leaders could make choices from the practical ideas for learning to create a discipleship, Confirmation or Lent course. Whoever is leading – preferably not alone – could plan to use both the chapters and the sessions to stimulate learning in the church community.

Acknowledgements

Many people and situations have had their influence on the gradual development of the work and insights into Christian community living and learning from which this handbook has emerged.

We are especially glad to thank the church community of the parish of St Mary the Virgin, Monkseaton, for collaboration, encouragement and prayer. As companions in planning and refining the shape and text of this Confirmation and discipleship handbook, we particularly want to mention: the brothers at Alnmouth Friary, Rachel Bainton, Robin and Katy Bell, Benjamin Carter, Brother Damian ssf, Dianna Van De Veldte, Philip Davies, Claire Greenwood, Dorothy Halliwell (Sue's mum, who taught her always to 'Say it as it is'), Richard Hart, the hospitality of Holy Island, Alan and Christina Kerkstra, Carole Lax, Eric and Carole Lewis, Don and Sylvia McDougle, Pat, Julio and Suzanne Moran, Sue Morgan, Pearl and Edward Newton, Eileen Noble, Jeff Pickering, Jo and Ruth Porter, Alison Stroud and Jane and William Walker.

Our thanks go also to Ruth McCurry of SPCK for her critical support and practical wisdom, and to the Venerable Sheila Watson, a past deaconess at St Mary's, for her Foreword.

Being God's People

Introduction

Travelling together differently

In touch with our deepest source

All life, created by God, is designed for and works best in community. God constantly regards us and the whole creation with love. The Church has the extraordinary gift of the Eucharist through which to show the world its true life. Two of the most striking acclamations in the text of the Eucharist are: 'The Lord is here!' and 'Great is the mystery of faith'. What powerful and outrageous claims, that when in gathering, singing, speaking and moving together, we become contemporaries of Christ, drawn more deeply into God's life and future hope for creation.

In the eucharistic drama, through singing, silence, adoring, beseeching, reading, sharing embrace, praying, offering money, bread and wine, eating and drinking together and going out, we learn to take part in communicating God's passionate work for the transformation of the whole of creation, including ourselves.

Christian communities need to be joyfully and seriously lit up. We must be evidence of God's presence, as pillars of fire on a desert journey (Exod. 13.21–22). We must communicate what we have experienced of the transformative power of true community, built on faith in the gift of God's love.

The world needs faithful and life-giving church communities, offering gifts for the life of the world. The baptized, gathered around Christ, flourish when worship and learning is how we do church together. Relying merely on the clergy and other leaders to be faithful on behalf of all has been one of the Church's sustained faults.

> **❝** I maintain that what sustains human life is a pattern of practices – good ways to relate to one another, honed in community and developed by tradition, learned from apprenticeship and embodied in habit. **❞**
>
> (SAMUEL WELLS)

> **❝** Now there are varieties of gifts, but the same Spirit; and there are varieties of services, but the same Lord; and there are varieties of activities, but it is the same God who activates all of them in everyone. **❞**
>
> (1 CORINTHIANS 12.4–6)

> **❝** If there's nobody home, it will be apparent, no matter how many lights are on. **❞**
>
> (BONNIE THURSTON)

1

Now is the time to be roused from sleep, recognizing ourselves boldly as communities of worshippers, disciples, leaders, evangelists, prophets, witnesses and learners. New Testament writers remind us that whatever gifts we have are for mutual service in urgently building Christian community that turns back all that is a rejection of the Gospel (1 Pet. 4.1–10 and 1 Cor. 12.12–31).

Nurturing an emerging future

Positively, we are offering here a Christian consciousness that:

- we are one with the whole of humanity – seeing in others the presence of the risen Christ;
- each person has equal dignity, as created by and alive with God's Spirit;
- Christian 'tradition' is a living, growing movement that responds to changing circumstances and patterns of living;
- there are many ways to be a Christian disciple;
- God works in networks of love and mutuality, beyond the confines of rigid religious patterns;
- we are invited to follow Jesus in his being one with the Father, 'Abba', as we pursue our own faith journeys;
- we can follow Jesus' way of serving others as friends or as neighbours, losing ourselves to find our own lives.

But for this we have to become disturbed.

The God of Scripture invites us to stop keeping God's holiness at bay. For example, we are called to cross the Red Sea to know release from slavery (Exod. 14.21–31), to receive water from a rock in the desert (Num. 20.1–13), to enter with hope in God into the Jordan to know we are beloved by God (Mark 1.5 and Josh. 3) and to receive the living water that is Christ (John 7.38). Our calling is to risk becoming more intimate towards God, one another and ourselves as a deep characteristic of what we call 'church'.

Navigating a complex and rapidly changing world is possible for churches, as public bodies in the world, because the risen Lord walks with us on the journey. In every generation, previous forms of church simply wear out and need to be replaced. What we did yesterday was great and valuable, but what the Holy Spirit calls out of us today is even more important.

Churches first need to honour in each place the real situation and people we find here. After honouring what is, we are truly free to move on to wherever God is calling us. Our personal realities may include disillusionment with our lives through illness, bereavement, failure to meet our own standards, broken relationships, and with the Church's attempts to provide a framework for knowing God. Jesus Christ, as someone born in a Bethlehem stable, in his ministry of friendship to those in dire need of healing and hope and in his despised crucifixion, is a reminder of God present to us often through the trials of human living.

Organizational development theory and practice helps us to learn how, in times of turbulence and systemic change, leadership comes from all levels, not only from 'the top'. When innovation derives from *speaking* and *doing* things differently, not merely *discussing* ideas from a distance:

Conversations that matter

In preparing to be a leader or participant in the conversations suggested here, consider how effectively core aspects of your own church's life are handled at present. How far do they create and present you as a community of the resurrection? How far do they invite participants to be broken open, to be drawn into this new life that is a new creation, a complete break with all that has gone before? See Figure 2 (overleaf).

How fully these elements of community living thrive when groups meet to talk, eat, pray, enquire and share life together (Matt. 18.20). God in Christ for our salvation not only came into our history as human but in situations of human weakness and vulnerability. Jesus showed how we can find God most easily among the 'poor'. He showed how to give unconditional support to

❝ Do not try to call them back to where they were, and do not try to call them to where you are, as beautiful as that place may seem to you. You must have the courage to go with them to a place that neither you nor they have ever been before. ❞

(A RESPONSE BY A STUDENT TO VINCENT DONOVAN)

❝ Christian ministry is the public activity of a baptized follower of Jesus Christ, flowing from the Spirit's charism and an individual personality on behalf of a Christian community to witness to, serve and realize the kingdom of God. ❞

(THOMAS O'MEARA)

❝ leadership comes as people start to connect deeply with who they really are and their part in both creating what is and realizing a future that embodies what they care most deeply about. ❞

(C. OTTO SCHARMER)

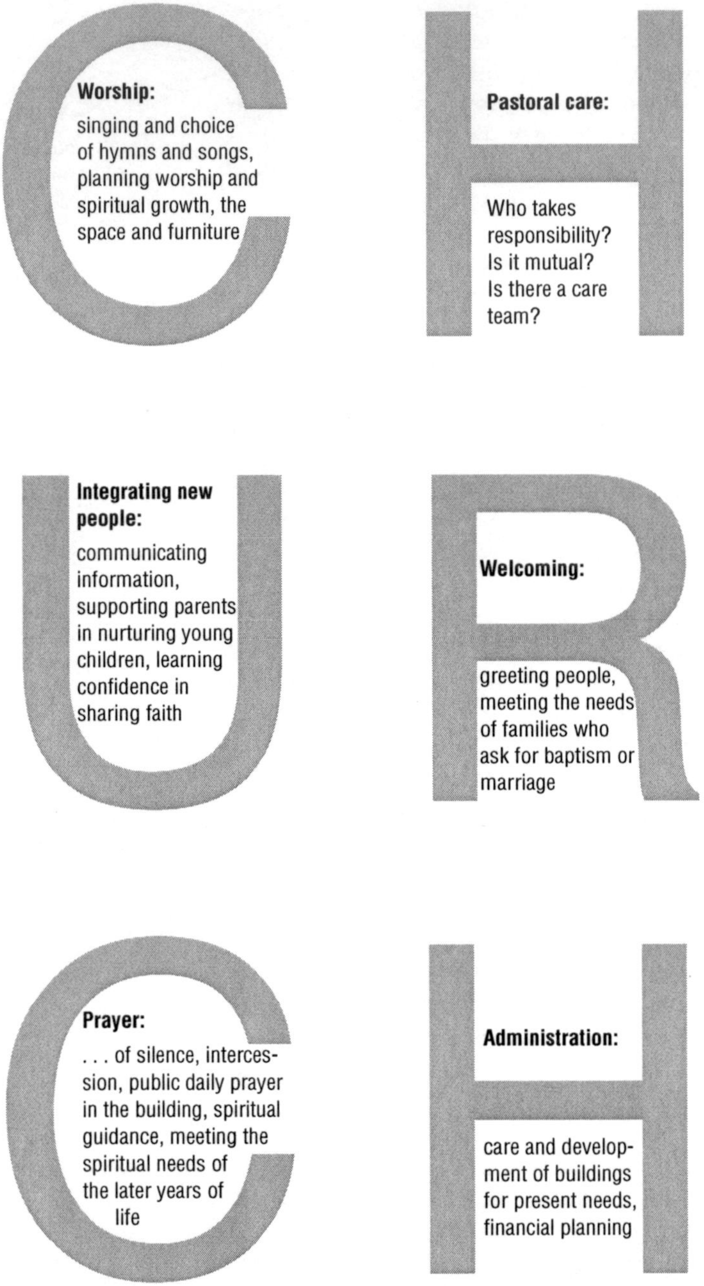

Worship:

singing and choice
of hymns and songs,
planning worship and
spiritual growth, the
space and furniture

Pastoral care:

Who takes
responsibility?
Is it mutual?
Is there a care
team?

**Integrating new
people:**

communicating
information,
supporting parents
in nurturing young
children, learning
confidence in
sharing faith

Welcoming:

greeting people,
meeting the needs
of families who
ask for baptism or
marriage

Prayer:

. . . of silence, intercession, public daily prayer
in the building, spiritual
guidance, meeting the
spiritual needs of
the later years of
life

Administration:

care and develop-
ment of buildings
for present needs,
financial planning

Figure 2: Aspects of church life

those whose lives are in pieces or who are marginalized by others. If we are to be a prophetic presence to lift the spirits of all who are imprisoned in some way, we must include *ourselves* among the 'poor'.

Travelling together differently

'Who is God?' is a persistent question in these pages. Of course, all our words are like dust in trying to describe God, but we can still try. For many centuries churches have behaved as though God were only 'changeless' and 'all powerful'. The long tradition of which we are a part also remembers that God is to be known in experiences of immigration, exile, bereavement, imprisonment, insecurity, struggle and tragedy. Often in our worship we exclaim: 'The Lord is here'; 'We proclaim the Lord's death until he comes' or 'God's presence is with us'.

Personally and as God's people we need to know God as closer than our very breath and to be known by name. Another contemporary image is that of conversation. Conversation values each person, explores difference, changes our viewpoints and behaviour and, most of all, allows each person to be carefully attended to. Then the impossible becomes imaginable.

> ❝ The biblical tradition says that truth is found not in abstract concepts, but in *an encounter with otherness.* ❞
>
> (RICHARD ROHR)

As one of another

Jesus calls us 'friends' who are known for our mutual love (John 17) and our willingness to show our vulnerability.

To a great extent we become who we are through the influence of others; all of us, without exception, can only follow Christ in companionship with others. Who we are as disciples and ministers is only possible when we let go of our need for control and success and go beneath the surface. As we learn to integrate our outer shell with our inner person, we learn better how to follow Jesus' way of mutual giving and receiving.

> ❝ In the midst of conflict, our question should not be 'Who is right?' but 'Do we believe?'. 'Faith is first, and the only one who is right is God.' ❞
>
> (BASIL PENNINGTON)

We believe that society now needs churches and groups of Christians who experience God's generous love and gifts. To the extent we allow ourselves to be converted or transformed, we can offer companionship and neighbourliness to others seeking to live in Christ.

To develop a Christian community through collaborative styles of ministry requires more than willingness or skill. Essentially it's an ethos or set of attitudes we need to be fostering that finely balances mutual respect and challenge.

What will this look like in a staff team, a church council, ministry or learning team?

It will be plain to all that the team:

- celebrates difference in temperament, ways of prayer and worship;
- respects each member;
- encourages honesty, not avoiding conflict;
- aims to avoid any sense of top-down delegation;
- chooses to be vulnerable with one another;
- recognizes the different scope of particular ministries;
- shares responsibility for keeping people together and watching out for one another (*episkope*).

The practical suggestions in this book arise out of various courses devised and tested in parish settings by us and our colleagues. We have found encouragement in hearing the experiences of participants; for example, Craig at an early stage of his journey reflects: 'Seeing and listening to the way people discuss their faith, and the variety of ways people live out their faith in Christ, is really helping me with burdens I am carrying in my own. To see the variety of ways of travelling has been very important to me.' We have learnt the value of meeting in different venues.

We have also been challenged in reviewing courses and have learnt to plan ahead more effectively through:

- fixing all dates before the course begins;
- booking meeting venues and the availability of hosts or visitors well before the course begins – and having a Plan B;
- planning with clergy and other church leaders when it's possible to have space in the Sunday worship and in the building, e.g. for exhibitions;
- arranging and confirming visits in advance, e.g. to a friary or a synagogue;

- stretching the course, with short runs of weekly meetings interspersed by gaps;
- keeping progress and planning meetings for leaders to manageable times;
- approaching administration connected with a Confirmation, e.g. checking baptism certificates, as soon as possible after the course starts;
- allowing rest time for leaders and also space for them to be fed, e.g. in Lent courses.

Not everyone you visit needs to be a Christian. Be inquisitive. Find out what people *do* believe and where they get their beliefs from. Don't be afraid to challenge them, gently, with your beliefs. Encourage the group members to ask the questions if possible.

Letting God's gaze transform us

Instead of muddling through to preserve the Church's status quo, even in the necessary structures of the institution, God's desire is that more and more we allow Christ's loving presence into our hearts. Gradually we can then choose to become vulnerably open to one another and to act collectively *as if*. That is to begin the journey towards letting what Jesus called 'The kingdom of God' become our default or overriding desire.

Formed by the Eucharist

There are many other tracks, but our chosen way is to act out, with our companions, a missionary community inspired by the Eucharist. Christianity is not a set of beliefs to be critiqued from an armchair as we pick and choose what will fit into our way of living. Rather it is a persuasive invitation to a way of life, offering hope and consolation, demanding our whole selves in just relations to all others. 'Double listening' is the nature of the church community's call. What we mean by this is that in every age the gospel emerges in new forms. Churches have to listen *simultaneously* in two directions. They need to be carefully in touch *both* with our deepest source,

Christ, *and* be listening to the cultures and locations in which our witness is set. Who lives and works here? What have we to learn? How can we be of service? A full account of a church community is offered where:

- God's presence is recognized in every part of the universe and human life and where disciples imagine how to co-create the world in the light of their knowledge of God's final purposes;

- the Eucharist, worship, prayer, healing, reconciliation and the expectation that all are called to maturity are ways of being contemporaries of Jesus now;

- the Holy Spirit is called upon to sustain faith and its sharing through listening, speech and action;

- attending to Scripture in many different ways resources faith and action;

- there is intentional conversation with those of different traditions, of other faiths and none;

- thought, learning, contemplation and a prophetic concern for God's creation and justice are interwoven;

- mutual structures for leadership and guidance echo the mutual, self-giving of God, lived by Jesus.

Priests, deacons, Readers and ministry team members share with the bishop in the oversight of the Church in its mission. Within local churches, often now in clusters, priests and other ministers are searching to know how to fulfil their particular office and task. Figure 3 shows how overseeing or watching out for (*episkope*), in varying circumstances, is a vital role and task for clergy and local ministry teams for the development of churches in mission.

When we succeed in modelling God's people in the light of the kingdom preached by Jesus, no one can be more or less. It's impossible to be more or less important. The value of all is equal even though the scope of our work will vary. But some have taken many years to prepare for public ministries and have made solemn vows before God, the bishop and the whole Church. In recent years, for the one leading the eucharistic event

❝ The Eucharist is a drama; it enacts the fundamental drama of all human existence. **❞**

(TIMOTHY RADCLIFFE)

❝ Paul envisages the local church as the body of Christ, as a charismatic community, where each member, by definition, has a function within the body, a role within the community of faith. **❞**

(JAMES DUNN)

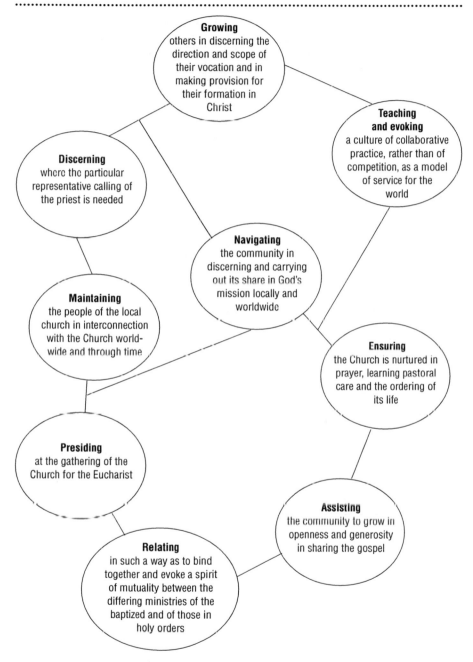

Figure 3: The tasks of a ministry team

the term 'president' or 'presider' has overtaken that of 'celebrant'. This is to remind ourselves that the 'liturgy' – meaning 'the people's work' – belongs to all the baptized, so that all are celebrants. The ones who preside are those ordained by the bishop and licensed for the time being as 'presider' within the mission of the local church.

Those who are confident and sensitive within the presider role and who can pray within it, have a sense of freedom, judging how to move aptly between order and spontaneity.

To share in leading worship is to have the privilege and responsibility of creating and holding together an environment that can at different moments become joyful, wild, passionate and unconditional in our love for Christ. We might think of their distinctive clothing – albs, stoles, chasubles – not in terms of status and separation but as giving the wearers 'permission' to inhabit their full role with confidence, to be a focus of unity and a support for the community daring to be stretched in faithfulness.

66 This is a meal for hungry people, for needy people, for people who are hungry for God, for love, for forgiveness, for acceptance, for peace. It's the kind of meal that both satisfies and promises more. It whets our appetite. 99

(DUNCAN B. FORRESTER)

As worshippers we are invited to move away from recognizing ourselves as solo Christians who may sometimes 'go to church services'. Instead we propose that, as God's people, in every fibre of our living, we *are* or *do* church (as a verb and not a noun). To talk about the 'shape' of the liturgy may seem a bit odd. But when we look at it closely, and perhaps especially when we visit other churches, even when the liturgy is in an unknown language we find that intuitively we know where we're up to. Of course, there is more to church than the corporate act of worship we call 'Eucharist' or 'Holy Communion', but all that we could want to say about being disciples of Jesus Christ together can be opened out and recognized in the sequence of the Eucharist, as outlined in the Contents page and on pages 24–5.

Each of the chapters and accompanying group sessions offered here relates to one or more facets of this eucharistic truth, which are outlined in the chapter headings of this book. Every chapter and accompanying session stands in its own right. The material provided for the group sessions is offered merely as a stimulus for leaders and participants to use as you will. They are an imaginative springboard or resource for reflecting: 'So here in *this* place what do *we* need to do and become to move towards a church where we become more truly present to God, to the world, to neighbour and to ourselves and grow creative leaders willing to stand up and take a full part?'

To become a community of Christian faith requires that we dare to let go of the past securities of buildings, furniture, hierarchies, familiar forms of worship, social confidence and all that hinders real contact with God and with neighbour. For a local church to grow in our present Western culture requires courage. It means taking up a clear identity without losing credible contact with those with whom we live and work. To be church now requires that we act *as if* God's future is already present and capable of being touched and known. When we respond in the Eucharistic Prayer to the outrageous statement: 'The Lord is here' with the preposterous reply: 'God's Spirit is with us', we are acting *as if.*

'Presence' on a personal and communal level is a theme very much in evidence in the disciplines of business leadership, education and psychotherapy, as well as in Christian spirituality. It is a clear reminder that God's people must find God's searching love in every part of nature and human endeavour.

To risk becoming a beacon of hope through this way of being church requires that *one or two* of the following characteristics may be found already in a few people who can be pioneers through:

- a willingness to engage in conversations where God and Jesus and the Spirit are spoken of in a natural way;
- holding a belief that all God's people matter and can make a difference;
- creating spaces where, in courtesy, we speak directly;
- offering worship in which different paths to holiness are regarded with respect;
- inviting gatherings where people's stories are heard;
- evoking attitudes of respect, so that the locality in

> ❝ Each of us is summoned by the creative God at work in the world to work with the Divine Artist . . . to create something of beauty as we process through our days and years empowered by the creative love of God to bring healing to our creative life. ❞
>
> (GORDON JACKSON)

which the church is set is not a problem, but a place full of God's activity;

- fostering a community life where people support each other in praying and meditating on Scripture in different ways;
- developing spirituality in which God is known in ordinary things;
- facilitating meetings where there is humour and laughter as well as lament and tears.

Learning together: ten values to explore

Affirmation

To give this course the chance to change your church, you definitely need the affirmation of your parish priest and church council. Without this there is a danger that the course could be just another thing that happens. It could even become divisive.

Spiritual seriousness

Expect new members of your church to be really interested in taking part and growing in faith. Lack of confidence and respect here results in churches closing down expectations and so losing energy.

Accepting our lack of knowledge

It's OK not to know everything and to ask what may seem stupid questions. Asking them helps everyone else.

Being real

Encourage everyone, including yourself, not to role play. Being as present as possible to oneself supports authentic learning.

Prayer support

Ensure that this course, and all those involved, are mentioned and prayed for by name at every opportunity. Expect the very fact that this is happening to add to the spirit of collaboration and zest of the church community.

Linking resurrection, mission and Eucharist

These ten short chapters and group sessions are to encourage us to be more innovative and imaginative as a community of the resurrection, formed for sharing God's mission through the disciplines and habits of the Eucharist. They support our learning about the shape of the Eucharist, how we shape our celebration and how our participation shapes our lives in Christ, *as one of another.*

Reflecting on experience

Starting from what we know and have experienced, we can be confident and allow others to speak from their insights too. Affirming what people offer in the way of comment is to be in the Spirit of Jesus who built his Church on Peter, with all the complexity of his enthusiasm and failure. Our aim is to grow together in ways of being human that are alive with God's glory.

Learning differently

A variety of learning styles is essential for a church community if it is to include a kaleidoscope of temperaments and people. All will be challenged by God through the material and by the engagement with others it entails. These sessions are equally for seekers and Confirmation candidates, as companions together. They combine reflection on Scripture, learning different ways of praying (through conversation and activity), ask how to be Christian in particular places and situations, and take seriously the experience, stories and views of the participants.

Relocating

A key to learning is travelling with questions. It's not essential, but the course will be enhanced if sessions can take place in a variety of places, sometimes beyond the church building, where people work or practise discipleship in the week.

Witnessing

Others, who may have been inhibited or prevented from taking part, will be watching carefully, and next time they may choose to participate. Experience shows that those who at first watch cautiously from the edge can often be drawn into fuller participation later. They may even be willing and able, eventually, to lead a session or a course or hear God's call to other ministries.

Preparing for Confirmation

People will take part in these sessions for various reasons, at every life stage. For those intending to be confirmed, we make a few practical suggestions rooted in experience.

- Invite the candidates to have a sponsor to accompany them through the course. Newcomers to church may be glad to be offered a sponsor from the community. Sponsors can benefit greatly themselves in this.
- Work out simply what is expected of sponsors during the sessions and at the Confirmation service.
- Ask for baptism certificates immediately as it can often take longer than you think to track them down.
- Add a session with your priest or Reader to reflect carefully on the words and commitment to be spoken in the Confirmation service.
- It's worth considering the benefits of running one or two of these sessions within a residential weekend at a retreat or religious house. The bonds between people will be much stronger if this is possible. This will take some forward planning and negotiation.
- The church needs to buy each candidate a gift, appropriate to each one, to help develop their faith.
- One evening soon before the Confirmation arrange a time of prayer when candidates, sponsors, close relatives and friends come together for a short vigil of preparation.

- Give shared energy to planning the Confirmation. What music and congregational involvement will there be? Make sure the candidates are able to stand to receive the bishop's laying on of hands.

- Create a memorable leaflet and have a good celebration in church before people go to their own family events.

- Arrange a session a month later for reflection and consideration of what gifts the candidates are deploying for Christ.

Setting up a group: practicalities

What leadership will you need?

The planning and running of the sessions need leaders who can act as hosts to the group, who can facilitate its learning. A great deal depends on the size of the church community. In many churches it may be that everyone does group planning and running together. In larger churches two or three leaders may be available. The commitment of time to doing this work thoroughly may mean a temporary withdrawal from other church commitments. Also, the degree to which medium-term and short-term planning is possible will be a factor in the outcome – it will not be possible just to pick up this book each time and use it.

If possible, have more than one leader and bear in mind the age and gender profile of the likely participants. At planning meetings follow the Rule of St Benedict in taking account of everyone present and in listening carefully to the youngest – they have much to offer. Make sure that one of the leaders has a particular role of looking out for people, watching faces and discerning issues. All those involved need to be cared for by those who take overall responsibility.

It's important that we move away from 'group discussion' to 'conversation'. An intentional move from objective discussion to holistic conversation and dialogue has characteristics such as:

- restoring hope for the future;
- finding joy in working together;
- discovering through conversations a greater wisdom that shows the path forward;
- finding courage in talking about what matters most to us;
- discovering a place where everyone is valued and anyone might contribute something that sparks the group.

So leaders act as hosts, creating a spirit of welcome where participants know they are truly wanted, greeted and appreciated. Leaders encourage listening, curiosity, the giving of careful attention to one another, laughter – and no one wanting to stop talking.

What title will you give this course?

Will it be 'Being the People of God' or something that works better for you? We've called ours: 'A Walk on the Wild Side'; 'Magical Mystery Tour'; 'Shock of the New'; 'Journey to the Centre of the Earth' – something that gives people permission to attend without losing their personality or self-confidence. Whatever you choose, make it engaging, current and inviting of curiosity. It pays to advertise. Think of ten imaginative journey titles . . .

How long will your sessions be?

Your sessions need to be about one and a half hours, no more – some people will have been at work or school all day.

Whoever is organizing the course needs to call together the team after the first session, halfway through the course and after it's over. Pastoral care and quality assurance need to be assessed so that adjustments can be made for subsequent courses. Nothing written here is essential, only the desire to bring people and the church community into a closer relationship with God and God's activity in the world.

The basic format is revealed through each session

Again, depending on the scale to which you are working and the confidence of the community, we envisage a small group taking overall responsibility. This group may or may not also be the leaders of the course. Ideally, group leaders, preferably working as a pair, will span the social profile of the church, with a bias towards those cultural and age groups that are under-represented. Experience shows the benefit of very different people travelling together. For some of the sessions, visitors may have an expertise that's required. Sometimes being hosted in other locations may be a creative possibility. Encouraging 60-pluses and 12-pluses to be companions on the pilgrimage is a reminder that the church community is uniquely placed to practise positively mutual relations. It's a test of our intentional gospel practice of radical difference in relation, a reminder of Paul's desire for respect between the various members of the body (1 Cor. 12.17).

Leaders will vary in their previous experience, and again we want to emphasize that these conversations are of a different order from head-focused group discussion, which can often leave many disempowered. In the planning process beforehand and between sessions, we envisage the leaders deciding how to use both Robin's and Sue's material. There are three parts in each of Sue's sessions:

1 What you need to do beforehand.
2 What might happen in the hour and a half.
3 What needs to happen afterwards to link with the next session.

Some of these actions are for leaders, some for participants. For simplicity's sake we've assumed that all the written material you need is contained here in the book – though you may sometimes choose to replace what is offered here with material more familiar to you. Sue has written earlier sessions quite tightly to enable leaders to grow gradually in confidence. As you progress you will need less of a framework and will be interested in trying out your own ideas.

Leader support

It's vital for the priest or whoever leads the church to endorse and encourage these conversations without necessarily taking part – regular contact is vital. The church council also needs to understand the importance of this work and, where necessary, underwrite the costs. By whatever means, refreshments, heating and space must be supplied – in generous quantities!

Tell everyone ten times in ten different ways

To get the message across, it may take several different ways of communicating that a group is forming and all are welcome to join. Standing up in church before the service or putting it in the notice sheet or the magazine will certainly have to be combined with a one-to-one approach. With flyers and timetable in hand, the leaders make individual approaches to all kinds of people. We have found that it can be quite unpredictable and often amazing that some are thrilled to be personally invited and taken seriously in this way.

No mere observers

All leaders are fully part of the group and offer their own vulnerability, within an agreed contract of confidentiality. Those leading groups also have the responsibility for watching out that the content and tone feeds learners of differing kinds, enough and at different moments. Creative skills should be encouraged, such as photography, painting, cooking, music or poetry writing. They may be a natural vehicle for some leaders through which to introduce learning that is a holistic and inclusive journey, deliberately turning away from being a group discussion.

Everyone is learning

Leaders and participants in groups will support one another in:

- **conversations that matter** – conversations on how to know, love and be addressed by God; on ditching inaccurate pictures of God; on deepening your experience of God the Father as always gently insistent, but with a patience inconceivable to us, that lets us absorb Christ into our lives at the pace we choose;

- **mutual care** – encouraging each other as pilgrims together and watching out if one goes missing;

- **encouraging risk** – so that all take a new chance for our hearts to be broken open to grow in love for Christ and in knowing his love for us; allowing God's love to be awakened in ourselves and those around us;

- **listening for God's call** – discerning what you need now (you can always return and read more another time); taking another step forward into helping the world by being part of a Christian community in your locality (Matt. 25.35–36 and 40).

> Trust the group and its leaders, stay with it,
> and share questions without anyone being left
> feeling stupid. If you notice people staying away
> from the group, take permission to make gentle
> enquiry while respecting their space.

Key questions for leaders

- How quickly can we begin now a group is ready to form?

- Who will act as administrator?

- What planning or permission is required?

- Who will devise the sessions?

- What hospitality will be offered?

- Can new people join in after the group has formed?

- What will you do if people who come to an early session then disappear?

- How will you respond when people get cold feet and express doubts of various kinds?

- How will the responsibility for a blend of challenge and care be exercised?

You will have other questions too.

Leaders will find the following Appendices on the St Mary's Monkseaton website, <www.stmarysmonkseaton.co.uk>.

1 Encouragement for communicating well.
2 Routes for letting God's word be present to us in Scripture.
3 Guidance on various ways of praying.
4 An exercise in self-awareness.
5 Course intercessions – an outline for getting started.
6 Words to resource conversation on 'Who is God?'
7 Guidance on talking with Jesus.
8 A course-evaluation example (also in Chapter 11 here).

1 Gathering in God's Presence

Crossing the threshold of becoming present to God, to one another, the world and ourselves

Stretching our imagination

A good deal of how we speak about Christian faith depends on imagination and the use of metaphor (Ps. 78.2 and Matt. 13.35). Here we are following the example of Jesus who:

- experienced God's presence and the work of the Spirit in a way that transformed all previous ways of believing and speaking;
- used many words, stories and images from his people's history and gave them a new twist – to communicate his experience and how we might share in it;
- used images from farming, nature, families, employment, finance and baking;
- offered the kind of 'knowing' that was more than information or speculation;
- offered, 'for those with ears to hear', an intuitive knowledge that somehow holds everything together so we can say, 'Yes, that's it; I want to give up everything else, in order to be part of that! Nothing else will satisfy!'

Through the eye of a needle

In many areas of life today, such as music, sport, art, medicine and education, the idea of 'presence' is often referred to as a vital ingredient for groups to move beyond an indifferent performance or interaction. Here's an example from the world of agriculture.

❝ If we are to learn to do the God–Self–Neighbour spiritual process as Jesus taught it, we must first learn how to move from the level of the physical and social to the level of the Mystery of Spirit. We must become adept at hacking metaphor. ❞

(JOHN SHEA)

A group of farmers met occasionally with a facilitator to discuss key issues in working together in their local area. On one occasion they seemed to be making no progress. New energy was released, however, when they chose to speak more vulnerably about their lives and the history of the land they were working. Once they became present to one another and to the location, they found a sense of a future awaiting them yet needing their fullest attention and connection if it were to come to fruition. They described beginning to act when inspired by that awaiting future as 'passing through the eye of a needle'. Their productivity increased in proportion to their putting their real selves into the situation.

This sense of presence emerged when the group members began to risk being real and authentic towards one another. They had at first been afraid and resistant, but eventually knew they had to cross a new threshold. One even spoke of having to 'die' in order to become part of the circle of people.

Through giving their disciplined and holistic attention, a new quality of space was able to emerge between the participants. This was described as a lack of judging, and instead an opening of eyes, heart and ears.

Resurrection: a new action by God

Jesus showed how to trust God's presence through healing, teaching and unbinding people from what gripped them, and his own willingness to embrace crucifixion and be raised from death.

Active Christian faith hinges on Jesus' resurrection from the dead. This fault line in history marks the beginning of the end. However things seem now, the amazing and unpredictable God of Scripture works now, in this world, inviting our co-operation and expectation of a world to come beyond our imagining (Isa. 49.8–16; Acts 10.34–43; Eph. 1.15–23). Instead of trying to fit Christianity into our existing lives, God invites us to re-imagine the world's possible life around the person, death and resurrection of Jesus Christ.

❝ Love grows . . . It receives and draws more strength. It is the same for ever, and it is born anew each day. Therefore this new life will also mean a new presence, and an endless leading into new truth. ❞

(STEPHEN COTTRELL)

❝ If I step all the way, it's such a relief to have taken the step. I feel freer. Somehow I didn't know beforehand that I would feel freer, even though I've done it before. ❞

(C. OTTO SCHARMER)

Jesus' death was not a story with a failed end. Jesus at his baptism, through the Holy Spirit, knew himself to be the Son of God, God's beloved (Mark 1.11). Mark, in his Gospel, wants us, like the centurion at the foot of the cross, to believe that Jesus truly is God's Son (Mark 15.39). When we believe in Jesus as the saving presence of God in our life and in the entire world, we too become God's daughters and sons.

Easter Day is the first day of a new creation. The Church shares in Christ's resurrection body. In the resurrection, the coming reign of God, which Jesus had proclaimed and lived, was now exploding into everyday living.

> ❝ What a God we have! And how fortunate we are to have him, this Father of our Master Jesus! Because Jesus was raised from the dead, we've been given a brand-new life and have everything to live for, including a future in heaven – and the future starts now! ❞
>
> (1 Peter 1.3–4, *The Message*)

Gathered to celebrate the Eucharist

Rather than offering a commentary on the Eucharist, here we're exploring key stages of it as an intense focus for our corporate sharing in Christian faith. At the start of a typical Sunday Eucharist in the Anglican Church there will be an entrance hymn in which the congregation sings God's praise and the ministers leading the service move to their places. Throughout this book we assume that the congregation are the celebrants, while an ordained priest, who shares in the leadership of the mission of a local church, 'presides'. Moving away from the term 'president', which in the world today presents mixed overtones, we're choosing the term 'presider'.

> ❝ Nothing states this fundamental characteristic of community life better than Mark 10:15: 'Truly I tell you, whoever does not receive the kingdom of God as a little child will never enter it.' This is not an invitation to childlike innocence and naiveté but a challenge to relinquish all claims of power and domination over others. ❞
>
> (KEVIN L. THEW FORRESTER)

As the hymn closes, the presider greets the congregation, probably saying a brief word about the theme of the day's readings and events and something important to the community's life. We've turned up from our different lives, in varying moods, with a handful of responsibilities, anxieties and things that are dear to us. Why have we come? What are we hoping to receive and intending to give? How do the leaders of the Christian community create a hospitable space into which we can all be gathered?

There's every sign that the competing pressures of weekend life have led many Christians to being at the Eucharist only when it's 'possible'. Life is hard for young

66 As a parent says, 'The one sure thing that will put Ben off church for life is to say, "You can't take part in the rugby tournament on Sunday morning."' 99

adults holding down a job with uncertainty about the world's future, paying a mortgage or rent or worrying about finding a life partner. And family dynamics are genuinely complex where rugby, swimming, music, illness, visiting the elderly or the grandchildren are vital ingredients of a full life.

Church councils constantly wrestle with their practical response to this situation. There have been eras in which church attendance had little competition for time on a Sunday, or when society and churches laid down penalties and guilt trips for non-attendance. We also know that church attendance can be something very different from being completely taken over and dislocated by God (Gen. 32.24–25).

What we are suggesting here is the slow building up within ourselves of a natural commitment, one that comes from a sense of yearning to be part of the eucharistic celebration – unless prevented by serious illness, work patterns, holidays or some unpredictable priority – so that it would be a source of sadness or loss to have been absent.

Experiencing Christ's risen presence

At one time church communities would so emphasize the importance of the 'consecration' of the bread and wine at the altar that it was forgotten that Christ is present through the Spirit in every moment of the eucharistic celebration:

- the gathering;
- confessing sin and being forgiven;
- attending to Scripture;
- confessing a common faith;
- the prayers of the people;
- sharing the Peace of Christ;
- praising God;
- giving thanks;
- remembering Jesus;
- opening to the Spirit;

- sharing communion;

- being sent out in mission.

So the risen Christ, living among us, meets us as we habitually bring into the present both God's past saving work and God's promised future.

Why the habit?

Although there is more to living Christian life than celebrating the Eucharist, there is nothing to which the shape and content of the Eucharist does not point. Key reasons for Christians choosing to be regularly gathered to celebrate the Eucharist are these:

The Eucharist feeds the life of the baptized community

God gathers us with a wide assembly of:

- the disciples sharing the Last Supper (Luke 22);

- those fired up to proclaim good news on the Day of Pentecost (Acts 2);

- Christians, in every time and place, filled with the same Spirit with which Jesus was baptized in the Jordan (Matt. 3);

- the communion of saints, angels and archangels and the whole company of heaven.

In order to:

- die to our own self-importance and learn to choose to live as agents of God's work in the world (Rom. ch. 6) . Unless we place God at the centre of our lives we end up there ourselves;

- pioneer a new way of seeing and living as neighbours and as equal disciples in which no one is dominated by another. This eucharistic community is more than an idea in the mind but acts like a midwife for a completely new reality (Rom. 6.3–5; 1 Cor. 10; Gal. 3.26–28, 5.24, 6.1 and 15);

- face up to baptismal challenges and responsibilities. We are co-workers with God to bring about, in

❝ This is the supper of the New Age, the meal of heaven, our tearful/joyful celebration today of God's tomorrow. We accept God's invitation to the feast and acclaim the coming victory of Christ. ❞

(DUNCAN B. FORRESTER)

❝ Every Eucharist is the sacrament of our home in the Lord, and yet breaks down the little home that we have made. We must throw down the walls that we build to keep out strangers. ❞

(TIMOTHY RADCLIFFE)

ourselves and the whole of creation, hope that without Jesus' resurrection would be impossible.

The Eucharist brings wholeness to the world through us

God gathers us into the company of those who, in countless locations, have celebrated the Eucharist. So we are connected with Christians in every part of the world who *now* are also gathered.

After Pentecost, empowered by the Spirit of the risen Christ, the earliest Christians began to celebrate the Eucharist. Early accounts tell of varying structures in different places. What they held in common was that by worshipping Christ in the Eucharist, their own way of seeing, and enacting their part in the world, was gradually transformed into God's way. As we celebrate Eucharist together, we are already part of God's promised reign, breaking through into the present.

- First, God is present to us, drawing us into the dynamic life of Trinitarian communion.

- Second, through the Eucharist, God draws us into God's own way of seeing and living within the life of the world.

In being attentive to God (in prayer, Scripture, bread and wine and silence), creation is revealed to us in God's way rather than ours. In meeting God we meet the world with fresh eyes (John 6.51.)

Worship and prayer bring the joy of knowing God's love and freedom

The Holy Spirit:

- stretches our sense of the greatness of God's love for us, so that we come to respond to that love;

- reconciles, inspires, deepens our faith and expands our sense of connection with other followers of Jesus;

- confirms us within corporate Christian identity, as God's people, grounded in peace and love, as well as disturbed to become more faithful disciples.

Consider the young man in Jesus' story who demanded his share of his father's money, squandered it and is drawn home as his only hope (Luke 15.11–end). The young man's father runs to embrace him in his crisis, delighted to have his son, without a word of reproach. So however perplexed or distressed we may be, worship opens our horizon to how God's future comes bounding forward into the present moment to meet the complex, murky, real person that we are now. God's Spirit breathes through us, transforming our present muddled ways of praying and living into the sharing of God's own life.

Health warning
But coming close to God, confessing our love for him in this way, is costly. Jesus asked, 'Can you share the cup that I drink?' To begin to share God's life is to take on Jesus' intimacy with the Father, which both made possible his works of love and self-giving but also brought crucifixion and the cry, 'My God, why have you abandoned me?' (Matt. 27.45–46)

Becoming children of another world
God gathers us:

* to be formed as disciples, both in ourselves and in relationship to the worshipping community;
* to have our imaginations fired through Scripture, prayer, mystery and presence;
* to start to see life with the eyes of God;
* to learn how all things belong together;
* to grow in the covenant of being God's co-workers, challenging exclusion and poverty and building justice and peace;
* to be released from our lesser agendas.

Churches practise community as doctors practise medicine. We are practising now, in advance, the kind of communion that Jesus promised will be finally true when God's kingdom comes in its fullness. This is what forms us as an intentional Christian community of the baptized (Heb. 12.22–24a).

> 66 We need to make time for God, jealously guarded time, in which we give loving attention to God, that the whole of our lives may be lived consciously as a loving relationship with God. 99
>
> (DUNCAN B. FORRESTER)

Notes for leaders: Session 1

Gathering in God's presence

What are you waiting for?

This session is about the beginning of the Eucharistic service – the part we call 'The gathering', where we are called together to meet each other in the presence of God. Who are we? What are we doing here?

Preparation: what needs to be planned in advance

Prepare for an adventure

For this first session we're offering detailed support, on the basis that as time goes on, leaders will grow in imagination and confidence to find their own way. Once you have the church's support for planning and offering this course, arrange an initial meeting of session leaders and those who will be taking responsibility. Pray that this course will enable everyone involved to become more present to God, self, neighbour, church and world. Read and reflect together on the introductory material on pages 1–20. We suggest that reading this book from start to finish may not be the best approach. Leaders, in planning a course, could start by browsing to see what most fits your situation. It might be a good idea to keep a notebook of decisions or points to remember, to help with planning subsequent courses.

We hope you're energized at the idea of accompanying a varied group of people on a journey of exploration into grown-up Christian faith. You may be keen to get started but at the same time be saying, 'This all looks too complicated' or 'too scary'. Feel the fear and do it anyway!

Sue, who has written the session material, has provided more than can be used in a single session. You're invited to make choices. At first you may want to follow her suggestions more or less as written, but once you find your feet you'll be able to adapt and be more creative. The aim is to support leaders, whose own growth in confidence on this journey is also an important part of the process.

Setting up the session

We are so used to gathering to watch or listen to someone else that learning to be part of the action means we have a lot of work to do. These meetings are not about technique but an invitation into a conversational way of being with each other that changes both our community and ourselves. Things to be considered in planning:

- [ ] For the first meeting, take great care to make a space to fit the group, probably in a circle, on chairs or on cushions, and choose a place that's a comfortable temperature.

- [ ] Arrive in enough time to make everything welcoming and to have a chance to catch up with one another and pray for those you are expecting.

- [ ] We know from experience that removing our shoes for some gatherings can help us to be more vulnerable. It might seem a step too far at the first meeting, but hold it in mind.

- [ ] Plan to share simple refreshments. Gradually encourage the involvement of the whole group in this but discourage competition in the standard of provision.

- [ ] Find a small table and place on it a cross, candle, Bible or Christian symbol, such as a fish, and perhaps a newspaper or object as a talking point. Over the course experiment with various translations of the Scriptures.

- [ ] Arrange lighting that invites people into the space – neither gloomy nor garish – and some welcoming music. Ensure over the coming weeks that you vary the music. Invite different people to bring or play music that is meaningful to them. Essential Christian community learning is appreciation of difference.

- [ ] Choose which readings will be used for the session and make enough copies. If possible distribute a colour picture for reflection. Make it small and beautiful. Suggest this could be left in the kitchen, perhaps stuck on the fridge – somewhere it may be easily seen. This could be a trigger for prayer until next time.

- [ ] Select which quotations from the chapter to use as conversation starters and mark them in your copy of the book for easy reference.

- [ ] Decide who will watch the time and ensure a good balance between covering the material, resourcing individuals and building the group.

- [ ] Recognize that in an hour and a half – the time to which people have committed themselves – it won't be possible to use all the material.

It's better to have some available that you don't use. Experience
will gradually help you decide when to move on. Have a strategy for
omitting material if time is running out.

The session in action

Being good hosts

For leaders and facilitators this is about ethos not activity. Acting
as hosts is a way of seeing the role. Are we truly ready to welcome
everyone who comes through the door with whatever they may bring of
themselves? Decide how to settle the group. Maybe make tea, coffee or
other drinks, and chat to help one another relax, despite the inevitable
anxiety. For everyone there'll be internal conversations going on with
questions like: 'What am I doing here?' 'What if they find out what I'm
really like?' or 'Will I be accepted?'

Lighting a candle

A leader might light a candle on this first occasion, others doing so at
later sessions. This is the first and simplest act of being part of a group.
It's also the easiest way for someone to acknowledge the presence of
Jesus, light of the world, without the embarrassment of saying anything.
This is holy ground for conversations that matter.

Does everyone know everyone else?

A good way to start might be for people to chat in pairs – and then for
each person to be prepared to tell the group three things they've learnt
about the other person. It doesn't need to take long. Depending on the
numbers present, allow five to ten minutes.

> Check that everyone has the same view of the confidentiality of
> the group: you can take away what you learn about God, yourself
> and how to live well, not what you learn about someone else.

Introducing the theme

Leaders explore what group members have made of the chapter that
goes with this session. Discuss what immediately stands out. A key
theme might well be 'being present to God' or 'God being present to us'.

Going a bit deeper, what does it mean that God *is* really here? Where would we look and how could we discover God together?

Don't be afraid of simple language. Keep it short. Make sure everyone feels comfortable to speak or to be quiet. Don't fill up silences by talking yourself – monologues are boring and create dependency.

Discussing the theme (Presence)

A leader tells the group which sentences or quotations from the chapter stood out especially for him or her. The group members are encouraged to do the same and perhaps read one or two sentences out loud.

This conversation has the capacity for creating the group and is about being honest and real, straightforward with God and with each other, letting that reality into all our life situations. It's about daring to be open to growing together. Don't be afraid of silences as people process internally.

Recall the story of the farmers (page 22) and how they could only make progress when they were daring to cross the threshold of being present, rather than seeing one another or their common issues from a distance.

Some questions you might ask

Note that questions count as they are open invitations for people to bring out ideas and to exchange possibilities. Expect to promote a conversation that is attractive, engaging and that breaks through previous assumptions.

- Can anyone recall having a creative experience of presence at work, with friends or anywhere else?

- Is there anywhere in particular where you feel totally present to yourself, others or God?

- When have things you decided to do been influenced by your sense of God's love? What difference did it make in terms of what you did and how you did it?

We can start from the assurance that all of us are known to God who loves us beyond measure. Together let's take another step in discovering who God might be and what God is like. Jesus, of course, is the best clue we have. Jesus came from God to show us who God really is. In Appendix 7 on the St Mary's, Monkseaton, website <www.stmarymonkseaton.co.uk> are words that might give us some clues.

Reading: 1 Peter 1.3–4

A leader reads this passage and then someone else reads the passage again, perhaps from *The Message* version of the Bible, as quoted earlier (page 23). Keep a two-minute silence while people digest it. Then ask, 'In what we just heard, what stands out for you?' 'What surprised you?' Suggest that people pick out favourite words, lines or visual images that the words bring to mind.

Affirm *everyone's* contribution. Let different people read it a couple of times again.

Now choose one of the quotations in the chapter, such as from the writing of Shea, Scharmer or Thew Forrester. Read it aloud, hold a silence for a minute and then share which phrases catch the imagination of group members.

Developing the theme

How is the risen Christ present today among us and in this particular place – right now?

The group could read headlines and photos in a newspaper, magazine or comic, asking, 'Where are you, God?' Rip out images or words and stick them up or lay them on the floor for all to see.

Leaders will start people talking about what they have chosen. Everyone can affirm each other's contributions.

Leaders – be willing to answer questions like, 'If God's everywhere, why does he let bad stuff happen?

Christ present in the Eucharist

In this chapter (pages 24–5) Robin introduced the celebration of the Eucharist as the way *above all* in which for 2,000 years Christians have known and spoken about Christ's presence. His presence in the Eucharist is a sign of his presence in every part of life, whether joy or sorrow, peace or distress.

Which ideas in the chapter on the Eucharist have the power to open up possibilities for us and for our church and world? Consider the ways in which choices have been made about your regular church's way of performing the drama of the Eucharist. As much as any words spoken, the movement and actions and who does them tell us who we are, as a community. So perhaps for the first time consider the choices your local church has made about how you celebrate the Eucharist. They will include areas such as:

- **Welcome** Are children and young people evident? Who is 'allowed' to participate?

- **Praise** What possibilities do we have for music and drama in various forms?

- **Active or passive** Are we creating a sacred space that holds together our experience of God as the Holy One and as our closest friend? What are the occasions when we are mainly expected to receive?

- **Growing in maturity** How is the whole person engaged, not just in mind and speech? Are there times when worship includes both gravitas and humour, sacrament and humanity? Is it a good balance?

- **Contributing to the welfare of our neighbourhood** Where are the places where we're making a genuine connection between gospel and world?

Gradually through this book we shall explore the pattern of the central Christian service all over the world in every language on every day. Some call it Holy Communion, the Mass, the Lord's Supper or the Eucharist. Our preference is for the latter. Refer back to the chapter headings of the book as a reminder of the overall shape of the service.

Shaped by Christ in Eucharist and the everyday
A leader helps the group find a way of voicing how:

- God is present everywhere in life and in the world.

- God is present in every part of the Eucharist, from the greeting to the dismissal.

That may draw out further conversation, especially for those whose personal or family life is at present very painful. Mutual care now and the offer of further conversation after the group meeting may be fitting. Now the group begins to take leave of one another.

Prayer
To pray in a group will be familiar to some and scary for others. Following the spirit of hospitality that has already begun to develop, trust and affirmation will be key. One who took part in such groups says:

> I talk to God as I'd talk to you now. The Bible's hard to work
> out and religion seems to be a lot of gobbledegook. It frightens

most people off because you can't understand it and what they're trying to get across. If you think about it, and you went to an ordinary Sunday service at a church anywhere – you'd be frightened to death.

(Bev Collett, course participant)

Here's an exercise that can encourage group prayer and can be adapted according to your circumstances.

Take a box of objects of various kinds:

- Ask everyone to choose one and spend a moment or two looking at or holding it.
- Suggest that each place his or her object in the middle of the space.
- Pray around the circle so that people know when it's their turn.
- Start each short prayer with a given phrase, such as, 'I thank you, God, today for . . .', inviting the group members to complete the sentence (with, for example, 'for recovery from illness' or 'for the love of my family'), to which the others respond, 'Lord, you hear our prayer'.
- Let those who don't wish to speak pray quietly as they put their object at the centre.
- End by saying together the Lord's Prayer and 'Lord, you love us and we are your people and you hear us'.

Taking leave of one another

- Ask people to discuss, in twos and then in the whole group, whether they can find any words to describe their experience. Reassure everyone that there's no hurry and that it's better to be real than rush into using other people's words about God that don't feel right.
- Everyone receives a copy of any poem or reading that has been spoken to take home.
- Next time, where are you going to meet and at what time? Anyone need a lift?
- What is the theme for the next session?
- Ask people to help organize refreshments.

- Can one person volunteer to do the short opening prayer, light the candle and be prepared to read a Scripture passage?
- Leaders must be prepared to stay behind until all have gone in case anyone needs to have a final word.

We leave one another in saying together a simple and familiar prayer called the Grace (2 Cor. 13.14). New Testament writers remind us that as God is generous, so God puts into us real power, gifts and inspiration. Help everyone to be confident in saying together and learning the words of the Grace as often spoken in public by Christian communities. As the group says the words quietly together, you may wish to include everyone by meeting their eyes in the group. There's a strong tradition too of marking ourselves with the sign of the cross in saying the Grace (see the note about this in Chapter 2, page 40).

> The Grace of our Lord Jesus Christ and the love of God and the fellowship of the Holy Spirit be with us all, now and always. Amen.

Leaders' reflection

Between sessions leaders will need to meet and several dates will need to be planned in advance to be as sure as possible that they really happen. As you progress you will develop your own questions and ways of reflecting. The following questions may be helpful to start with:

- Practically speaking, what went as you intended – or not?
- Who didn't come and what action will you take?
- What struck you most about the first session?
- What did you learn?
- What seems to be missing?
- Can we go to a deeper level?
- Who needs special care?

2 Given a New Start

Believing good news and getting a new life

Made for one another

As a baptized and baptizing community, our calling is to demonstrate how God loves all creation unconditionally (Luke 15.11–32), always yearning for our deeper response. We are invited to step out of the prison we make when we refuse to be present to God, to others and to ourselves.

Being gathered to God brings consolation but also a testing of our living (Ps. 50). Jesus challenges our small horizons and encourages us to enter into a new relationship with God who:

- is in love with us and delights in us his creation;
- longs to bring out the best in us, so that we shall be able to accept ourselves, forgive and accept others and desire their fullest maturing;
- we can call Abba – Daddy – who is closer to us than our breath;
- frees us from fear (Ps. 139.13–16).

Who is God?

In worship we often say, 'Glory to the Father, and to the Son and to the Holy Spirit'. Variations include speaking of God as 'Earth-Maker, Pain-Bearer, Love-Maker' (*A New Zealand Prayer Book*). Identifying God as 'Trinity' is the way that Christians, over centuries, have distilled our experience of God, the relational mystery of love, as

66 What the church owes the world is what the church has been given, that is, the privilege to be a community capable of confessing our sins before God and before one another. 99

(STANLEY HAUERWAS)

mutual communion. Everything that has been created, loved and is on its way to completion in God is part of a whole, rather than isolated. This changes everything about how we see the world. Now everything is seen to belong and to affect every other part.

We live among so many who do not really appreciate that they are loved or lovable. We must recognize ourselves among them. The sacramental and human life of the Church reminds us that God is with us in all our fragility, *really present*, the source of truest life.

Relationship restored

After the Gathering, the second key event in the Eucharist is the confessing of sin and receiving forgiveness, sometimes called the 'Act of Penitence'. Self-examination and confession are clearly an important aspect of our growth as disciples. But it's easy for this act to become so routine we hardly notice it. We can help ourselves by reflecting on our lives before we come to the Eucharist, precisely why today we need forgiveness and healing.

Wrestling like Jesus

We know that Jesus, in planning his mission with the Father, went into the desert for 40 days and 40 nights (Mark 1.12–13). He inspires us to dare to enter into spaces where we can listen to God and grow in intimacy with our Father in Heaven. We know that Jesus was tempted to take shortcuts with cheap miracles or, later, to avoid the hard road of the cross. We will often find God telling us what we would rather not hear.

Jesus shared our wrestling with temptation in the humble way in which he joined the repenting crowds being baptized by his cousin, John the Baptizer (Mark 1.9–12). All through the gospels we see Jesus' character being stretched to capacity in body, mind and spirit in his relationships with disciples, friends and enemies. Like us, Jesus had to work out appropriate ways of being friends with and of expressing his sexuality among women and men in the community, especially those with whom he worked most intimately.

> 66 God does not settle for mandated or fear-based relationships, but rather desires willing and free relationships with 'friends' (John 15.15). It is called 'a new covenant' (Jer. 31.31; Luke 22.20), but one that is a quite new and unbelievable possibility for most people (1 Cor. 13.12). 99

(RICHARD ROHR)

> 66 Time comes tense, edgy, rimmed by tragedy, edged by all our deaths. 99

(CATHERINE KELLER)

A popular caricature of church life is that we come to services just to be told off for how sinful we are. But the first recorded words of Jesus in his Galilean mission invited people to wake up to the urgency of the time, believe good news about God and see things from a completely new perspective, and turn around or get a new life (Mark 1.14–15).

Radically, he invites us to revisit our whole take on life. The gathering for the Eucharist is much more than a mutual support group, rather a place where God comes with healing and transforming presence to sweep away our old certainties and securities. Yet although God wants to remove our hearts of stone, the free choice is ours, and the long process of conversion is, for most, a painfully slow journey of being persuaded to let go of what we believe we cannot live without. Until we know God's love we shall hang on to alternative sources of comfort.

Letting God become our Lord

The confession of sin has always been a key part of Christian worship. The benefit of bringing into words our failures and inadequacy is to grow in honesty with God and with ourselves. Personally and corporately we are accepting, despite every defence and excuse, that our lives are not yet ordered in the form of God's final purposes for us. To reflect on our lives and recognize our failures is the first step towards growing into communion with God and with others (Isa. 55.8–9). Letting God be our primary attraction, our north star, the community confesses its sin and receives forgiveness, knowing God's presence within the brokenness and trials of our everyday life (see Figure 4).

Jesus taught his disciples that to have life is to lose it and that we may enter only by a narrow gate. Celebrating the Eucharist reminds us that we are constantly in danger of being formed in patterns that are too small, narrow and unjust to be owned by Christ. Scapegoating from the community those we believe are particularly evil contradicts Jesus' way of radical inclusion. We need to recognize how often sin and brokenness is a characteristic of the entire community or network of which we are a part.

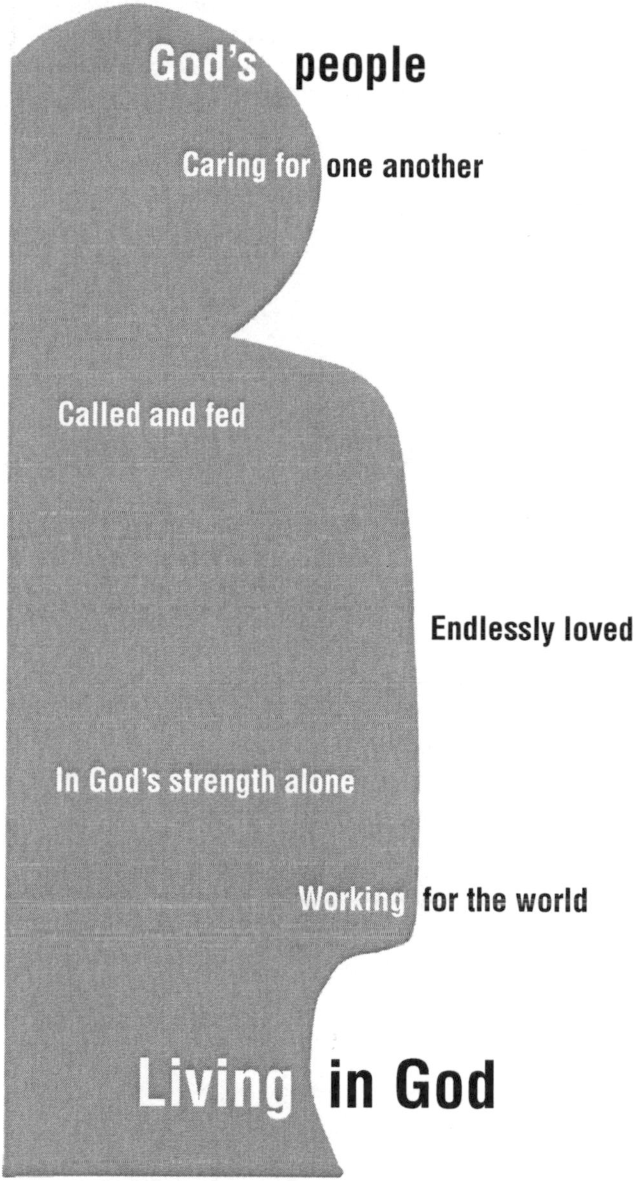

Figure 4: God's people living in God

Making the sign of the cross on our bodies

The cross is God's sign of love – a love that gives everything. As a sign that God's forgiveness is indiscriminate and overtakes our sinfulness, some Christians make the sign of the cross on their bodies when the priest announces God's forgiveness, 'In the name of the Father, Son, and Holy Spirit'. It can become a powerful ritual so long as it remains a mindful act. Carefully, with our forefinger, we trace the symbol of God's overcoming death and evil from our forehead to our chest and from left shoulder to right and back to the centre. We ask God to bless our whole person.

- As an act of faithful courage, we touch the forehead and chest. In the Eastern Christian tradition this is to open the brow and the heart as centres of vision and compassion.
- According to Jewish wisdom, as we briefly but definitely touch the left and right shoulders, we activate the spiritual foci of mercy and strength.

At the point of receiving forgiveness, hearing the gospel announced, before sharing the bread and wine and as you receive the final blessing, explore this bodily action – for a trial period of three months – and only then reflect on its value for you and whether you would wish to stop.

Called to live

Forgiven, we stand ready to hear what God asks of us or wishes to give to us now God has called us by name, knows our every thought and still loves us boundlessly. Free of guilt, we may hear some particular calling that is new to us within our ordinary lives.

Forgiveness that brings liberation

Jesus was unpopular with religious leaders of his time because he saw sin not in terms of rule breaking but as a failure to recognize that God's love is always seeking human response. His parables urge us to let go of the proud fantasy that we are perfect, or of the despair of thinking we are a hopeless case. Accepting pardon for our own weaknesses, as a basis for our maturing (2 Cor. 12.10), shows we have confidence in God's power (2 Cor. 4.7) and are willing to live in God's word about us rather than our own.

Like Jesus we are called to be children of a Father who regards us as 'Beloved' (Matt. 3.17). To accept and be thankful for God's loving forgiveness is the road to being generous in our forgiving of others. But forgiveness doesn't come naturally to most of us. 'An eye for an eye' holds a deep attraction when we manage society from our perspective (Matt. 5.38–42).

Jesus had a particular ministry to sinners and others excluded from the community. He was adamant that to follow in God's way of love excludes communities violently pushing people out in order to feel secure. The one thing that Jesus excludes is exclusion. However, he is not condoning the tolerance of abusive relations, whether in child care or international relations. The person who has been at fault has to recognize that scars remain and a new way of relating has to be worked for. Rather than withholding forgiveness or seeking vengeance, Jesus invites us to the practice of non-violent ways of taking away the offender's power to continue hurting others.

The Passion of Jesus

This truth about a compassionate God was shown most starkly in the conversation between Jesus and one of those crucified with him. In response to the criminal beseeching Jesus to 'remember me when you come into your kingdom', he gives the clear assurance, 'today you will be with me in Paradise' (Luke 23.42–43).

The cross was 'hell' for Jesus. His intimate relationship with his 'Abba' in his work for the sake of what he called God's 'kingdom', the ultimate shape of love, inevitably brought him to final conflict with threatened authorities. Although he knew his Father's love he also experienced excruciating pain, utter disappointment, dark despair – even abandonment by God. The bottom line in receiving Jesus' assurance of reconciliation is that

66 The church envisaged in Ephesians sustains human dignity without excluding anyone; its ethic of reconciliation faces religious, racial, cultural and household issues; it advocates an array of neighbour-friendly virtues; it encourages learning and teaching; and it sponsors high quality, respectful communications as an alternative to violence. 99

(DAVID F. FORD)

there is no hellish place to which God has not already been.

Christian communities that go beyond merely secular ways to model God's abundant compassion do so because they have outdistanced the formalities of religion. They have found a depth and a passion (contemplative action) through letting God form their words and actions. For this to be possible, the eucharistic community needs to be sinking deep prayer-wells into God's presence and love.

Notes for leaders: Session 2

Given a new start

Want a new life?

This session is about the second stage of the Eucharist, where we stand before God and say we are sorry for all that we have done wrong. We do this in penitence and in sure knowledge of forgiveness. We thank God in the Gloria.

Preparation: what needs to be planned in advance

Leaders will have met for reflection on Session 1. In looking towards Session 2, encourage one another by revisiting the principles and material in the introduction to Session 1 (pages 28–30).

Summarize what you feel confident about from last time. In the light of experience, what will you especially want to make sure about in planning Session 2?

Setting up the session

For the second session we suggest you meet in the same place and at the same time as for the first. This will help develop a familiarity with each other without having to worry about the environment or how to get there.

The theme of this session is penitence and reconciliation. Decide which parts of the chapter to use on receiving God's loving forgiveness and avoiding living with a permanent sense of guilt and unworthiness.

There are some obvious helps in the bullet-pointed section on page 36. We suggest that you make those a key focus this time, asking group members to find connections between the points in the chapter, Scripture, hymns, prayers and their own experience.

You'll need to make sure everyone has access to the text of the chapter. One of the leaders needs to be ready with some suggestions to foster conversation.

Leaders are encouraged to vary how things are arranged. Keep a sense of order but also suggest movement forward. Having a Christian understanding of God's way of dealing with violence between nations, communities and individuals is one underlying intention of this chapter. A second is to help people know God's word of unconditional love towards us, rather than common notions of punishment, retribution and violence. One possibility would be to make a focus for the meeting that could include objects such as a travel case, stones, handcuffs, sticks, objects or images of things associated with violence. Leaders may wish to develop this to offer something that best fits the situation and the possibilities on offer. The opening worship can be based around this display, including the 'presence-of-Christ' candle (see page 30). Check who agreed to light the candle, to lead a prayer and read the suggested passage from John below.

The session in action

Remember the task of being hosts as people gather (see page 30).

Lighting a candle

The group circles around the focus for worship, such as an open travel case and a pile of stones. A leader explains that as each of us offers a prayer, we will put a stone in the case.

The group then calms itself by keeping a short silence. Members could be invited to still their bodies by noting any aches or pains, breathing and heartbeat rhythms and mental or emotional processes – see the notes on silent prayer in the Appendices. Leaders invite someone to light a candle as a sign Christ's presence among us. A simple prayer is offered by the person who agreed to do this at the end of the last session.

Getting to know one another better

Refreshments are available as part of our mutual welcoming.

To continue forming the group and recognizing that people will have forgotten names and are perhaps embarrassed by that, try something like: 'What made me really cross this week was . . . And what I did about it was . . .' This is light-hearted, and especially helps younger ones see that all have issues to deal with, no matter how outwardly confident we may seem.

Invite any comments or continuing thoughts from the time since the previous session. Remind each other what the last session was about. What made you laugh last time? It's OK to enjoy the group. Thank and affirm one another.

Check – again – that everyone has the same view of the confidentiality of the group: you can take away what you learn about God, yourself and how to live well, not what you learn about someone else.

Introducing the theme

A leader begins with a few points s/he wishes to draw from the chapter. This is also a chance for anyone to say what struck them in reading the chapter and to make a bid for that issue to be included at some point. Encourage people to grow together through helping them to listen well. Some may need to be encouraged to speak less often to allow others in.

Get a life: some questions you might ask

- What does it mean generally when you say 'get a life'?
- Specifically, what does it mean for Christians to 'get a life'?
- Where do these overlap and where do they differ?

In the conversation let everyone speak. The leaders, rather than providing answers, will try to open up the questions further.

Experience forgiveness

Leaders invite the group to look again at the chapter and to find a phrase or idea that speaks to them especially. If the group is large, break into two halves for this. Then go on to invite the sharing of stories about forgiving or being forgiven.

Reading: John 14.6–12

Leaders will have asked someone last week to be responsible for reading.
   Let the words be read through slowly while everyone reads a copy. Hold a silence for three minutes. Ask anyone to say if a word or phrase stands out for them. When everyone who wishes has spoken, have the passage read again.

Developing the theme

Leaders may then invite participants to continue the conversation on 'Get a life' and the bullet points on this page, while also referring to the bullet points on page 36. What experience is there in the group of the new life that comes from the risen Christ?
   Describe the scene of a scuffle at the gates of heaven. Some are trying to see what is the hold-up, until people nearer the front, who can see

right through the pearly gates, turn in outrage, saying, 'Have you seen some of the people they've got in there? I'm certainly not going in if she's there!'

Further questions to explore
Does the group believe:

* that God never gives up on anyone?
* that God can change us, bit by bit, as over a lifetime we allow Christ to help us let go of what holds us back?

Or have members of the group different experiences or beliefs?

Responding to being forgiven
Can we feel released by God from what held us before?

Let's use our imaginations. How does it feel to say, 'Fantastic, thank you, I feel better now . . .' and, even better, stand with everyone and sing those words? Surely we need trumpets and drums and dance. In the Eucharist, to know in our whole bodies and voices that we are forgiven, we sing together the early Church's song, 'Glory to God in the highest and peace to his people on earth'. Here is the spontaneous outburst of a thankful community. Look at this in your service book and read it together or sing a version like the Peruvian 'Gloria'. Or provide some simple musical instruments, get people into twos or threes and send them to write their own 'Gloria' or look at some versions from Wild Goose or Taizé music resources.

Consider this passage, written by a family therapist, on getting in touch with feelings to create positive energy:

> In our present culture, where feelings are often suppressed,
> I certainly see value in enabling people to know themselves
> emotionally. Emotions get us going. They are the way we move
> ourselves from a stimulus to a response.
>
> (Gaie Houston)

Most of us want to be right again with God. When we are reconciled, we can peacefully move on to enquire what more God wants of us.

Prayer
The group circles around the focus for worship – an open travel case and a pile of stones in this example (see above). A leader introduces the

theme, inviting group members, in a short while, to place a stone in the case, symbolic of the burdens they are carrying today.

There follows a two-minute silence while people collect their thoughts and decide how to respond truthfully. Those who can, pray in words, thanking God for taking away from heavy things we've been carrying round. Others pray silently as they put a stone into the case. There must be room for anyone who cannot deal with this to take a short time on their own without any anxiety in the group.

At the end, as the case is full, a leader thanks God for taking all our burdens and forgiving us. We thank him for each other and for the chance, again and again to start out anew.

Leaders help the group to create a short prayer of thanks.

Taking leave of one another

- In twos and then in the whole group, ask:
  - What was most helpful in the session?
  - What was hard?
  - Will people be here at the next session?
  - Are there any other questions or issues?
- Distribute any handouts.
- Were any plans made for the group to make a contribution to worship this coming Sunday?
- Make arrangements for the next session's venue and how to get there.
- End with the Grace.

Leaders' reflection

Either now or in a few days, as arranged previously, leaders will pray together and ask questions such as:

- What went well or not so well?
- Any obvious remedies?
- Has there been a sense of enjoyment?
- Is everyone participating?
- Are we concerned about anyone in the group?
- Do they perhaps need a one-to-one conversation?
- Who will follow up anyone who was missing?

3 Attending to Scripture

Responding to the risk of God's
inexhaustible promise

Listening to God's word

After the Gloria follows a prayer known as the Collect, which literally 'collects up' the theme of the day as we move to listen to the Scripture readings and make our response to them.

Through Scripture we know the presence of God, not merely words on a page. The account of the risen Christ suddenly appearing to the astounded disciples (John 20.19–20) is a reminder of God's faithful yet unsettling presence in every time and place:

- constantly taking the initiative to be among us and in our lives;
- with us in Christ, who lived and taught us how to lose life in order to find it, suffered and was crucified (and still bears the wounds);
- comes close to reassure, calm fear and share peace with us;
- releases to us the gift of the Holy Spirit (as the risen Christ breathed on the disciples);
- takes us beyond any previous experience – just when we think we have everything sorted, staggeringly, God invites us to be stretched to see everything from a new perspective.

God's word in the Eucharist, other forms of worship, study groups and in personal times of reflection brings God into our lives now. The narratives of Creation,

Exodus, Exile, Empty Tomb, Pentecost, and the experience of the first Christians are more than past events. They are scenes in which to know our own lives differently. The entire Eucharist forms us as a gospel-shaped community. Specifically, as God speaks to us through Scripture, we are built up in our:

- sense of God's character;
- personal response to God's purpose for ourselves;
- task of making the present world more transparent to the coming of God's future.

Food for discipleship

The God of Scripture is one who speaks to us (Heb. 4.12) and in speaking creates, nourishes and gives saving power. When Isaiah (55.11) refers to the Lord speaking, the prophet connects God's speech directly with what happens: 'It shall not return to me empty, but it shall accomplish that which I purpose.' What God intends in speech takes place in reality. Ezekiel was given a scroll of writing to 'eat' – or digest (Ezek. 2.8—3.11). Scripture, in telling the truth about God, tells the truth about the world and about God's desire for the quality of relationships between people and people and creation (Jer. 15.16).

Scripture shows us Jesus' forceful and overwhelming presence that nerves us to respond. He evokes in people the question, 'Who is this?' The Gospels say he *is* Lord and also one who *does* saving actions.

Letting Scripture shape us

Scripture comes to us in *our* place from many *other* places where it has already been. So we recognize that Christian living in a complex, difficult society is almost impossible without being fed by Scripture. When we stand to hear the Gospel in the Eucharist (or sit quietly at home reading from Scripture) we recognize we are being addressed by many other Christian communities who have gathered before us (2 Pet. 3.1–2).

> 66 The principal function of the Scriptures is to facilitate the re-enactment of Christ's story among his followers, in such a way as to foster the life, activity and organization of the believing community. 99
>
> (NICHOLAS KING)

66 Most of us, to put it rudely, need to shut up, to be silent for a while, to listen. And when we do use language, we need to use it respectfully. In the realm of prayer and worship, familiarity can comfort; it can also kill. 99

(BONNIE THURSTON)

66 O Lord . . . you know when I sit down and when I rise up; you discern my paths from far away. You search out my path and my lying down, and are acquainted with all my ways. 99

(PSALM 139.1–3)

66 Do you have eyes of flesh? Do you see as humans see? 99

(JOB 10.4)

66 And everyone who has left houses or brothers or sisters or father or mother or children or fields, for my name's sake, will receive a hundredfold and will inherit eternal life. 99

(MATTHEW 19.29)

Scripture is not there for us to judge or to choose only the bits we like. It asks questions of us. We are not simply deciphering the ancient text to see what can be made of it and whether it might be relevant or useful today. Rather than reading just words on the page we eagerly expect the *presence* of God to work in and through our imaginations, stretched beyond our usual beliefs about who we are and what we need or desire.

We normally use the Church's 'lectionary' (plan of readings that covers most of the Bible over a period of time) as a counter to our inventing our own version of faith. Absorbing God's word, we ask searching questions about the values, ethics and assumptions of human organizations, government and Church.

Conversations with those who do not share our faith can enrich our own understanding of Scripture. We no longer justify slavery, witch-burning or apartheid from the Bible. Nor do all Christians draw the same conclusions from what they read. How open can we be to others in their refusal to accept some Christian conclusions about Scripture and gender, sexuality, power, leadership and hot issues in society and politics?

The word in *this* place

The following verses, and the longer text that surrounds them, open up a recognition that faith is never in the abstract but comes enmeshed in the everyday. God comes to us as our own lives. God is present to us within the intimate detail of our humanity.

God who comes to us in Jesus pitches his tent among us. All reading of Scripture takes place somewhere (John 1.14). Scholars used to offer impersonal readings of Scripture that were assumed to be just 'normal' and free of bias. Understanding Scripture does need the expertise of those who have spent a lifetime studying language and the history of religious thinking. But let's also notice how many other parts of our common knowing need to be confidently included, as mutually enriching. Potentially, all the places shown in Figure 5 are where we encounter the all-seeing God of Scripture.

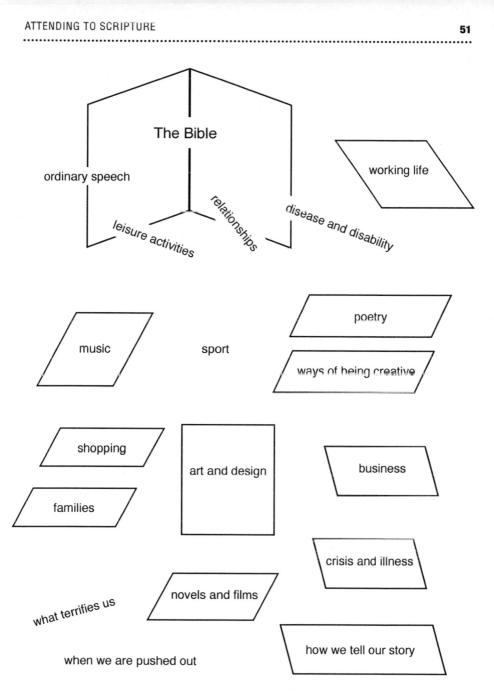

Figure 5: God in the whole of life

66 none of you can become my disciple if you do not give up all your possessions. 99

(LUKE 14.33)

66 You know that it was because of a physical infirmity that I first announced the gospel to you. 99

(GALATIANS 4.13–15)

66 In the end be as creative, imaginative, experimental and adventurous as you can! Discerning 'the word in place' is a calling with multiple avenues of possibility. 99

(LOUISE J. LAWRENCE)

66 I am puzzled about which Bible people are reading when they suggest religion and politics don't mix. 99

(DESMOND TUTU)

66 The Bible becomes God's word (not just a pious book) because it vivifies, enlightens, contrasts, repudiates, praises what is going on today in this society. 99

(OSCAR ROMERO)

'Contextual Bible study' originated in the tensions of apartheid in South Africa and has now become a major source of Christian wisdom. It is a method that gives priority to local experience and culture as the place for knowing God's presence as 'being with others'. In challenging accepted attitudes and political regimes it has brought many individuals and communities into danger and death.

Archbishop Oscar Romero, who in 1980 was martyred for speaking out his concerns about the conditions of the poor in El Salvador, interwove what he learnt through contemplating Scripture with what he learnt from listening to the Holy Spirit in the joys, hopes, grief and anguish of local communities. On Sundays, often having prayed with Scripture through the night, he spoke of God's presence in the events of the previous week. He spoke in a Christmas sermon of Christ's birth, connecting it with the abductions and tortures that were daily occurrences.

In Western society now Christian faith is gently mocked, even though televised documentary and fictional accounts of the puzzling lives of clergy can still fascinate and increase the ratings. Some speak of the Church today living in exile. The prophet Jeremiah (ch. 29) insisted that in Exile God's people must maintain a faithful witness, re-learn their own faith and seek the welfare of the city where they are placed. Jesus invites us to be displaced as a way of meeting God (Luke 9.46–53). It's certainly a reminder of:

- the eucharistic community's important task of creating a good place with a hopeful story – within itself for all who come, and within its neighbourhood;

- the opportunity given to eucharistic communities to offer alternative possibilities of how life could be – both in word and in mobilizing action;

- the dangers for any Christian community that becomes so accommodated to its situation, dominant ways of seeing life and even a shared common purpose, that it has nothing extra to say;

- the need to look out for all those who have no place to call home;

- the dangers of Christians being too much at home in church;

- the urgency, when Christian faith comes back to town (Jer. 31.8–9), that the exile experience will have been for nothing if, when it was out in the wilderness where God searches for the sheep that has become detached, it didn't listen (Matt. 18.12).

Receiving God's word

Overflowing with flawed and wounded people, Scripture shows how we can become transformed sinners, making huge mistakes before we find a truer way. Giving disciplined time to hearing, reading and contemplating Scripture – in church, in a group or alone – builds up our sense of God working in our lives and in the world. Over a lifetime we can vary our practice of studying and meditating on Scripture to find what is most life-giving for us.

Rather than worrying about correct understanding with our minds, the priority must be to ask, 'Is my praying of Scripture deepening my relationship with God and solidarity with all in the world who are "poor"?' If the answer is 'No', then we should feel free to search among the many possibilities that have proved valuable to others.

> 66 this is the messy business of discerning the word in place: 'to start with the ordinary and the everyday, with personal life, with corporate stories, with "our times" in their political and social agony, is [likewise] the bold business of theology.' 99
>
> (SALLIE McFAGUE)

Notes for leaders: Session 3

Attending to Scripture

Risks and promises

This session is about the part of the eucharistic service where we hear from both the Old and New Testament parts of Scripture. With the subsequent reading of the Gospel in the midst of the assembly, we begin to see what a risky business it can be following God's word.

Preparation: what needs to be planned in advance

Leaders will have made plans before the course began, but now is the time to check that arrangements are secure. You may also wish to revisit some of the group-process ideas from earlier in the book. Also consider whether to offer a reminder of the confidentiality agreement.

This time you could devise a simple way of inviting the comments of participants for your reflection.

Someone (possibly a visitor or local priest or Reader) needs to be given the task of explaining about the different forms of literature in the Bible. Also the leaders may want to prepare the section in the chapter on seeing the God of Scripture in film or poetry, depending on where you are. You might want to show a few DVD clips – or find someone who can – so that you can reflect on God in routine as well as unexpected places.

Leaders need to give thought to the final prayers on God in the world.

Is the priest and congregation expecting some input from the group this coming Sunday?

Setting up the session

Although by now leaders will be flexing their wings, we offer again a structure for the security of the group.

Let's assume that several months or weeks ago you decided that this session would be out and about. This means your church will both be breathing *within* the life of your neighbourhood and breathing *in* the life of your neighbourhood. Sue offers here some pointers about making the most of sessions on other people's territory.

- This session could work well in the synagogue, local library or a creative studio for arts or crafts. Use your imaginations to connect God with ordinary living.

- In every place you choose, and with every person who has offered to help, give them a sense of the course. Explain that you're honouring everyone's lives as a place where God is at work.

- Check what arrangements need to be made for you to make tea and take biscuits and so on. Be prepared to be surprised by God, yourselves and your hosts. Show them this chapter and session notes.

The session in action

Introducing the theme

First, invite contributions on what from the chapter especially emerges for people. In small groups (or the whole group if you are small to start with), consider some of the key ideas, such as Scripture as food, as shaping the life of the Church, as a way of seeing God's work in the everyday and world politics. This can be linked to the actual place in which you are meeting as well to the places known to the members of the group.

It is an ideal time to make sure everyone has a copy of the Bible and has time to find their way around it. Leaders (or a visitor) need to be able to say something briefly about the order the books are in and the difference between the various kinds of writing. It's vital too for the group to see how many of the stories, such as that of Jacob, have a timeless message about how lives are changed when God's presence is recognized.

Now look in detail at the section of the chapter called 'The word in *this* place' (pages 50–3). Choose one or two of the points to expand on. Leaders could take one each and help the group to grasp what is implied and link it with their own experience.

Experiences of praying with Scripture

Experiences of praying with Scripture let our imaginations be unhooked from anything that limits them. This is God's presence being revealed to us. Invite the group to consider experimenting with one or two of the ways of praying with Scripture described in the Appendices. What support can the group offer its members for this?

Going deeper

In your conversations you might consider:

- When we celebrate the Eucharist, whose stories are included or excluded?
- Why is the gospel so important to us and what is the part it plays in our service and our lives?
- What part might we be playing in the gospel story?

Referring back to the Scripture passages on God knowing us intimately, the leaders help the group to pray around the theme of God's presence in the world and in the lives of people we know. End with the Lord's Prayer and a prayer offered by a leader.

Taking leave of one another

- Ask simply what clear memory each person will take home from this session. What has your host for the session made of it all?
- Invite members to take a few moments in the group to choose a way of living regularly with Scripture. This could briefly be revisited on a regular basis.
- Ask for a simple response from the group about what seems to be emerging.
- Are there any difficulties to be faced?
- Explain where you will be for the next session and at what time.
- Ask people to be prepared with a prayer or a reading for next time, and ask some of them to bring refreshments for taking on a walk.

Leaders' reflection

- What kind of environment are we creating?
- Is it working for everyone?
- What adjustments may be needed?
- If you planned ahead to make a link between the session and Sunday morning's Eucharist, what needs to happen now?

4 Celebrating Belief

*Confessing our belief with Christians
of every other time and place*

Confessing who we are – God's people

After listening to the Scripture readings and engaging
with the Sermon, the community stands to recite the
Nicene Creed (or another authorized creed). The Anglican Church – the primary Church for which we are writing, even though we hope we will connect with others
– has not laid too much stress on the detail of creeds as
definitions of belonging. Rather it regards a statement of
belief as a place to inhabit, given to us by those who have
been Christians before us, and where we are safe to ask
questions. We know that if any of us were asked to give
an account, for example, of our beliefs about resurrection, the variety would be endless.

Some find it irritating that we don't patrol sharper
frontiers between those who believe correctly and those
who don't. But Christian faith is not agreement to a set
of ideas or rules of behaviour. It's an invitation for the
whole of us, our 'heart', in many different situations, to
be broken open and transformed. Our model, always,
is the generous, open and loving response of Jesus in
his relationship with the Father. Jesus' parable of the
returning son is the touchstone (Luke 15 and John 4.34;
5.30; 8.28–30; 14.31).

Celebrating the Creed, spoken or sung, is telling out
together *not* whom we judge God to be but what God
in Christ, through the Holy Spirit, has made us through
his cross and resurrection. So God becomes present to
us, inviting as much response as we can offer today and
hoping for more tomorrow. To those who yearn for more
order, Jesus offers instead *presence*, a joyful surrender to

God in all the complexity of life, often without words. Our brothers and sisters are those who do the will of the Father (Mark 3.31–35; 7.21–23).

❝ The believer is always learning, moving in and out of speech, and silence in a continuous wonder and a continuous turning inside-out of mind and feeling. ❞

(ROWAN WILLIAMS)

Godly Play, a contemporary form of Christian formation often used with children but not always, is rooted in storytelling, wonder and creativity. It is a reminder of the humility, playfulness and imagination needed for our growth in faith. The destabilizing, pilgrimage invitation is to let God be the telling influence in our lives. Not knowing the road ahead or having certainty where it takes us is deeply inscribed in the Christian way of utter trust in God.

Joyful surrender

Jesus showed in healing actions his teaching that God's love is to be trusted if we make it the centre of a new life. Christian faith isn't *about* Christ but to be *in* Christ, like drinking wine rather than just reading the label on the bottle. We are a network of people who share a common baptism and faith in one Lord (see Acts 2.42, 44, 47).

❝ When his family heard it, they went out to restrain him, for people were saying, 'He has gone out of his mind.' ❞

(MARK 3.21)

Saying or singing the Creed in the Eucharist gives us a familiar safe place – see Figure 6.

It is personally costly to make as a priority in our lives a belief in God, with whom we can be in intimate relationship and who calls us from the future to be, here and now, agents of how things will be when God finally has God's way with us. For all of us this means detaching ourselves from being overcome by cynicism, criticism or alternative beliefs of family and friends. Jesus is our companion in this struggle. Considered unstable by his mother, family and disciples, he remained true to his constant relation with his 'Abba'. Like him, our vocation is to be sons and daughters of our heavenly Father.

❝ When the days drew near for him to be taken up, he set his face to go to Jerusalem. ❞

(LUKE 9.51)

❝ Because of this many of his disciples turned back and no longer went about with him. ❞

(JOHN 6.66)

Figure 6: A safe place for exploring

❝ For all who are led by the Spirit of God are children of God . . . When we cry, 'Abba! Father!' it is that very Spirit bearing witness with our spirit that we are children of God, and if children, then heirs, heirs of God and joint heirs with Christ – if, in fact, we suffer with him so that we may also be glorified with him. ❞

(ROMANS 8.14–17)

Classical Christian language of God as Father and as inevitably 'he' in our present Western society holds both reassurance and exclusion for people. In this book we have largely avoided associating God with purely masculine pronouns. We are glad to associate ourselves with those who search for ways of knowing and speaking of God that go beyond limiting God to the traditional categories of Father, Son and Spirit. In this book, however, we have chosen to stay with classical language rather than to speculate with alternatives. Conversations around these thoughts can be woven into any of the sessions.

Doubt and faith

Every sentence of the Creed is a variation on the idea that the God that Jesus shows us is God-in-relation and God-in-love with us. The constant invitation is to let go of pictures of God that are inaccurate, lack the capacity to feed us or are just too small: a lifetime's work.

Experience and biographies show it's quite usual to go through times of confusion or not knowing what we believe. Having a spiritual guide or soul friend can be very helpful as a support to keep our heads above water at such times. These relationships, properly, have a mutual benefit.

Belief – always a view from a point

Creeds map a highway along which the Christian Church has chosen to travel and to which we are invited. It gives us a shape, direction or compass bearing. Of course we can spend a lifetime struggling and questioning, especially when faith is stretched to the limits by experiences and events.

No one believes it all and no one believes it all the time. But these beliefs are not so open that I can say, 'I'm a Christian' when I choose to ignore completely the contours that the words outline. To recite the Creed is a way of humbly saying, 'We belong to this network of those who have navigated belief before us.'

Illness and emotional suffering will affect our faith. We can be bitter and outraged that God could allow tragedy to happen to ourselves or someone close. There is a long Jewish tradition that it is our right to argue with God and that God can take any anger we could ever muster. The God of Scripture cries out with the poor and oppressed, showing solidarity with suffering victims. God's hope for the world is shown when children are nurtured well, older people live in dignity and there is peace based on justice (Isa. 65.20–23).

It seems that God is showing us that anger is the normal, healthy and essential companion of hope and compassion. If we're not angry enough to work for the possibility of another world, we're not following God in caring or being immersed in the world's suffering.

> 66 let us never doubt that we too, like Abraham and Moses, may argue with the Lord. It is our right. 99
>
> (NAOMI ALDERMAN)

When, personally, we're facing the worst situations, we may need to rely on God's own anger being present and to join in. Shouting at God on the beach or in an empty church may lead to the recognition that God is present, already lamenting and crying with us. We have no need to protect God from our anger.

God knows what we're facing; in Christ's crucifixion and every form of human abandonment, God is already present and suffering. We may fall into God's hands, despite everything (Heb. 10.31), as there is nowhere else to go. The desert of doubt has often been the place where people have grown into an adult faith, leaving behind what they learnt as children.

> 66 My God you can torture me to death but I will always believe in you: I will love you always, even in spite of yourself. And these are my final words my God of anger: you will not succeed in making me deny you. 99
>
> (JOSSEL RACHOWER)

An act of courage

The God in whom most people say they can't believe:

- seems incredible after Auschwitz;
- gets the blame for natural disasters, such as earthquakes and tsunamis;
- is accused of cruelty when we see our life partners or friends die prematurely;

> 66 To recite the creed is courageous. We are exposing ourselves to accusations of being naïve, bigoted, arrogant and credulous. 99
>
> (TIMOTHY RADCLIFFE)

- seems bizarre when you look at the Church's organization that seems to prefer men to women and rich people rather than poor.

Despite the labours of Christian thinkers down the ages, the idea persists that Christians believe in a God who is like a President with unlimited power. Who then is God? Christian belief sees in the way the world works and in the way Jesus does God's work a mutual relationship within God that we call Trinity. This is a very different belief from that popularly rejected – the old man in the sky who rigidly and arbitrarily controls, at will.

In the light of the Trinity everything looks different. Mature Christian friendship with the Trinitarian God is to believe that the world is filled with the loving mutuality of this God. This belief changes our perception of everything and everyone and the relations between them.

Most people will never read the Bible or look at the Creed. When people see gospel-shaped relationships in community they have a clue about the good news. The God of Jesus invites us to demonstrate forgiveness, reconciliation, diversity, respect and inclusion.

❝ truth [may be seen as] that indestructible life that is open to us when we cease to live as private and self-determining individuals and enter the communion of the Church's life, which is also the communion of God's own personal life-in-relation. ❞

(ROWAN WILLIAMS)

Expecting all things to be made new

The Creed comes to us, like Scripture, through the centuries. It's a wager, an offering, a commitment that we make to being present to ancestors of the faith and those who celebrate the Eucharist now, in many different places. The early centuries of Christian faith are littered with strife, often very bitter, such as over the detail of beliefs about whether Christ was really God.

People who leave church often do so out of boredom. Our celebration of faith can be too thin, grim or worthy. To speak or sing out the Creed as a poem of praise for God's work among us is the way to know the vibrating presence of God in worship. The Christian belief in God as Trinity is a way of saying that God, who is passionate, outgoing love, shows in the face of Christ and in the work of the Holy Spirit what it means to connect with God in the whole of life.

The God of Jesus insisted that in the coming reign, new household rules would apply – the coldest would sit nearest the fire, the hungriest would be fed first and the poorest would pay the least. Whatever relationships or questions we have in the world's life are most truthfully known in this revealing of God and in God's work among us. This is God's plan for everything in heaven and earth when all things are gathered into Christ and God is given thanks and glory (Eph. 1.3–14).

Reciting the Creed is the amazing task of God's people. In the eucharistic worship of this household, God and creatures meet and prepare for the time when all will fully be united in God's life.

❝ From birth to death, in sickness and in health, in joy and in grief, people have celebrated this supper. Families, communities, nations have re-enacted this supper for tragedy and for victory. In refugee camp and in palace, in country kirk or great cathedral, in prison chapel or at sea this meal is celebrated . . . one great community in earth and in heaven. ❞

(GREGORY DIX)

Notes for leaders: Session 4

Celebrating belief

Nobody believes it all

In this session we consider the Creed. Saying or singing it is one thing. Believing it can be quite another.

Preparation: what needs to be planned in advance

Today could be an 'off the premises' visit, so leaders need to negotiate advance plans for an interesting venue for exploring belief. This session on belief tells us who we are as God's people. Take some time to consider ways in which belief can lead to our being joyful. Talk around these and find out what they could be in practice.

The Scripture passages in the chapter focus on the invitation to be children of our Father, working through the Spirit with Christ. Do we have a sense of being God's children? Do we behave as if that were true? Do we really believe God loves us?

There are lots of ways you could take the group, bearing in mind that you'll be on the move and may need to find one or two stopping places. Does anyone have a problem with walking and need a different exercise – and who will stay with them?

Some conversation starters that may help include:

- Which phrases or ideas in this chapter most connect with you?
- Is there anyone in the group who has never doubted their belief?
- In our society now, what is needed most from Christian community belief and living?
- Are we scared to make it known that we are regular attenders at the Eucharist and read Scripture and pray?
- What does our family make of our doing this course?

Was it agreed with the priest and local church that next Sunday would include a slide show either in the worship or at refreshments after-wards? How will this be interpreted to the community?

Have you chosen Scripture passages and readers?

Copies of the Creed you will say together need to be provided.

Setting up the session

Sue's favourite is to go together on a walk with cameras (this will probably have to be daytime). Take as your photographic brief, 'Where is God in all this?' Find many things, places or people that God loves and works with. One of the group or a friend will later need to help download these images to a laptop for the community to see on Sunday.

Before setting off on the walk, find a place to gather. It may not be possible to light a candle. What could you focus on instead to remind the group of Christ's presence?

But first ask the group what they learnt last time. Are there any ideas to share? We grow together through being comfortable enough to pray and share confidences together. Let God in on the work.

The session in action

If the circumstances of where you're meeting permit, keep up with the pattern of candle, prayer and food.

Plan beforehand who will read from Scripture some of the passages referred to in the chapter. They illustrate what is possible when our lives are transformed by knowing the depth of God's love for us.

Introducing the theme

Perhaps start with the proposal that 'No one believes it all and no one believes it all the time.'

Consider how Christ is present in unexpected places.

Prepare the group to expect to be surprised on the walk.

Using the notes in the preparation section above, leaders can be imaginative in supporting conversations that encourage everyone to share ideas. On the walk, above all encourage one another to be imaginative and confident in this activity. Take pictures from strange angles. Go slowly enough as if you were preparing to paint the detail. Ask yourselves where is God here and here and here? The canvas on which we are living is the whole of God's Trinitarian life in the whole of the world and our everyday lives.

Exploring the theme

If you can stop for a rest and share refreshments, do so. Either then or after the walk, open up some of the ideas in the chapter, perhaps with these questions:

- As a believing community, what have we received from those who have gone before us, to which we sign up each week in church?
- For us personally, what are the hardest parts of belief?

In order to prepare to share the photographs with the church community, what will need to happen quite urgently and who will be involved and when? If you're showing these pictures on Sunday, how will you introduce them? Perhaps by asking, 'Where is God' in familiar, comfortable places, at school or college, in the doctor's surgery, on the motorway, in the shopping area, at places that are neglected or dangerous to us, on a playing field or a park, by a river or seaside – the huge variety of places and people where God creates and makes new, hour by hour.

What does it mean on page 63 that we believe in God's world made new? Read Ephesians 1.3–14 putting into words God's promise that in the end all will be made well despite appearances now. What could this mean for places and people and churches that at present are having a tough time or not reaching their full potential? Is God's power really greater than all the forces of evil and damaged humanity?

Going deeper

Find a place where, slowly, standing in a circle, the group can read together the Creed regularly used on Sundays. When anyone has a problem with a phrase or sentence they stand a little outside the circle but continue to say the Creed with the others. At the end, first in twos then all together, share questions or interests. If possible make a record in some way. With the photographs on Sunday, show these comments to the community in church.

Taking leave of one another

- Listen to this passage read aloud:

In worship we enter God's world, a world of mystery. But we are not escaping from this world, with all its ambiguities, conflicts and suffering. Worship is also a stage, so that others may see, in what we say and do, a little of what the kingdom of God is like, and be invited to join in a role in God's great drama.

(Duncan B. Forrester)

- Say the Grace together.
- Make arrangements for the preparation of the photograph display.
- Explain that the next session will be at church.
- Check who will pray and offer to prepare refreshments.
- Invite everyone to read Genesis 28 before next time.

Leaders' reflection

Leaders should briefly review this session and make careful plans for the photography display and interpretation.

5 Calling on God

Praying that God will stretch our imaginations and take us beyond our human capacity

God in the rawness of life

Christian prayer inherits the Jewish expectation that, in utter dependence, we can turn to a merciful God. For example, read in Exodus 2.23 how prayer is a howl of despair from desperate slaves. The book of Psalms reminds us that we too can expect our cries of praise, lament and need to God to be heard.

Jesus' ministry shows God's response to those who know their need:

- The urgent expectation of a blind beggar (Mark 10.47) who repeatedly cries, 'Jesus, Son of David, have mercy on me', expecting to be healed.
- The widow who wouldn't give up her demand for justice until the court granted her petition (Luke 18.1–8).

The prayers of the people

The entire Eucharist is prayer, God's active relation and presence among us. But after the Creed comes the specific time when God's people turn to God with urgent requests. Prayers for others spill out from our own gratitude for being co-workers with God who works for the world's perfection.

We're showing how we have heard God's prompting to join him in active compassion for the needs of the world, the Church, our neighbour and ourselves. Our requests arise out of need and the expectation that God will answer. We can be obsessed by shaping the prayer correctly, the ways we present them or by struggles with the sound system. The prayers need to be heard against the backdrop of being present to God in urgency and in a desire to see the world renewed. Imagine if, sometimes, those who are able were to stand and prayers were encouraged to arise from all over the church, even if we couldn't always catch all the words.

What we gain from our Jewish forebears in faith is the expectation that when we pray:

- we listen for what we believe is God's will for others and then ask for it;
- we awaken a gift in ourselves to serve the need of those for whom we pray;
- God will indeed be roused – though in unpredictable ways;
- we are challenging our own depth of compassion;
- we are including ourselves among the 'poor' (in whatever sense), rather than praying for 'those who are poor';
- we are opening ourselves to the widest canvas of God's purposes for the whole creation – beyond our imagining.

> 66 According to Jesus, the concern of the Spirit of God was to speak for the poor, for the victims of cruelty and systematic injustices, for prisoners, the sick and those locked out of any meaningful participation in society by bars of ignorance. 99
>
> (MUSIMBI KANYORO)

Playing a musical instrument requires dedicated routine practice. In this way people recognizably become musicians. Prayer as an end in itself is a vital part of discipleship. In systematically taking time to pray we become more and more exposed to God's ways of working and grow in desire to become part of his loving intentions.

Praying within the locality

Jacob in his dream of a ladder going between earth and heaven reminds us how God's presence is available, wherever and whenever we turn to God. Moses at the burning bush gives us the insight that every place is holy and that God supports every effort to bring freedom to the oppressed.

In every local church a ladder of prayer exists so that God is utterly present in any moment when, simply, we turn to God – just as we might to a friend. Church communities, just by existing, can reveal God's presence and God's desire for truthful action.

The prayer that the visible local church people and building carries is a patchwork of shopping, child-rearing, job-seeking, marrying, mourning, being born and growing older, learning and loving. Whether notable or ruinous, the church building in stone or bricks and mortar is a sacrament of God's desire for the flourishing of all creatures.

The connection between the place of baptism (font), the place for reading Scripture (ambo or lectern) and the table for the bread and wine (altar) needs to be given careful thought. They tell us, often more than any sermon or explanation, of what is going on here.

It matters that we keep God's holy place beautiful, clean and uncluttered. The Holy Space should hold in tension God's utter distance and intense friendliness, as a sign of all the connections we make between eucharistic worship and the lives of people – in joy and sorrow.

The clergy, Readers, wardens, administrators, vergers and flower arrangers are all guardians of a place that can make the entire locality one in which God is naturally encountered. Routinely through baptisms, weddings and funerals, and in critical times of abductions, murders and flooding when flowers are laid out and vigil candles lit, the parish church is holy ground, a place of radical hope.

Wherever there is a Christian community, a gathering of Christian people who pray, together and alone, on behalf of the world and the neighbourhood, however we struggle and fail, they make a difference. What would it take:

- for more churches to be open much of the time?
- to have a place for those in trouble to write a prayer or light a candle?
- for churches to be known to be available for peace and silence?

❝ The interior of the church has been arranged so that a wide elliptical space in the centre invites the congregation to gather round the ambo to listen to the gospel reading . . . The church has become a place of movement and communal assembly. ❞

(JEAN-MARC FURNON)

❝ give thanks to these unknown people, who often go round with great respect and attention, for the truth that they make us feel, strangers that we are in this place, a resting place in our journey. ❞

(FRANÇOIS MARTY)

- for people to know they could quietly slip into a chapel and weep?

- to be safe in church to struggle, with no one to inter-fere – though with obvious clues for where to turn for support?

Notes for leaders: Session 5

Calling on God

Are you stretched in all directions?

After the Sermon and Creed, the presider introduces the prayers
(intercessions) of the people. These prayers are offered to the Father, in
the power of the Spirit and in union with Christ. Ideally they will have
been prepared and spoken by one or more members of the congregation,
from within the body of the church.

Preparation: what needs to be planned in advance

Use the last session's photographs to help you see who or what needs
the church's prayer. You may like to check again the notes on being good
hosts and confidentiality from Chapter 1. Take time to reflect on
what you see happening here, and how far these conversations are
fostering a sense of community. Careful preparation will allow the
leaders to develop some of their own ideas on intercessory prayer.
Ideally, group members will have also read the chapter beforehand.

This session will be in church. Does your building have a relaxed
and intimate space? What rearrangements of furniture might improve
things?

A leader will need to be prepared to offer the final prayer.

The session in action

What will you choose as a centre for reflection in this session on
intercession? A newspaper, a cross, a string of prayer beads?

Praying as God's people

On this occasion, along with a central candle representing Christ's
presence, each person has a candle to show how, as part of Christ, we are
in solidarity with one another and the world. These could be lit as people
check in with one another and say how they are. As the theme this time
is intercession, invite people to take a few moments to think whom or
what to pray for. God's people are not a closed community but connected to all the places and networks of God's world. Write prayers on

coloured cards shaped like a fish or a cross, and place them around the candles. Two or three moments of silence could be held. These candles could be kept and placed on the altar in church on Sunday, with a brief comment from the presider.

A leader could offer a prayer based on a real situation in everyone's mind today.

Are there issues from last time? How did the photographic exhibition go?

Introducing the theme

We are listening to God and God's work among the people and situations of the world, so that our prayers follow the grain of God's desire. On a large sheet of paper write down the words or issues that come to people straight away about intercession. Refer to quotes from the chapter.

Scripture readings

Have one or two voices slowly read the account of Jacob's ladder in Genesis 28.11–19.

Focus carefully on verses 16–17: "'Surely the LORD is in this place – and I did not know it!" And he was afraid, and said, "This is none other than the house of God, and this is the gate of heaven."'

Discuss:

- Where are there places or moments in which the group members have especially experienced God's presence?
- Which were the times when you had little or no sense of God's presence?
- Was God absent when people most needed God?
- What makes you angry with God?

Also read John 1.51 – here is a clear reference to Jacob's dream and a pointer to Jesus Christ as the one in whom especially we can know God intimately: 'And he said to him, "Very truly, I tell you, you will see heaven opened and the angels of God ascending and descending upon the Son of Man."'

Opening up the themes

To intercede is to recognize that between us – God's people – and God there is a constant ladder of conversation and presence, a two-way relationship in which we both receive as well as send. In this session the

group will be asked to prepare intercessions for the following Sunday
in church – with proper negotiation with clergy or whoever is normally
responsible.

- Let the group spend a moment considering our prayers as rungs on
  that ladder – perhaps even representing it in some way.
- What will the group want to pray about especially at this time?
- What makes God angry in the world today? Are we angry about this
  too? Which parts of Scripture seem most to connect with this loving
  concern? How does anger get transformed into action?

The Eucharist is the central way in which from the very beginnings of
the Church the Christian community has prayed and learnt to pray.

Group work – the brief

You have been asked to prepare the intercessions for Sunday-morning
worship. You have been given the chance to do it 'your way' and
challenged to be as imaginative as possible.

An idea to play with

(Allow about half an hour – the leaders can develop this as seems best.)

- To connect well with the photographs taken in the previous session,
  arrange a slide show of them or a display. Let everyone ponder them
  carefully and discuss them. Gradually write down or speak out
  where prayer is needed or thanksgiving arises in response to the
  photographs. Consider how to develop this for use with the
  congregation.
- Now everyone gathers for refreshments and reviews what they have
  been doing, receives encouragement and takes another look at the
  original brief.

The next question is how to bring together what has been discovered
and expressed for the Eucharist on Sunday so as to stimulate and
support the prayer of the whole community.

- Ask each person to show or explain what they have been working on.
- Choose a few sentences from the text of the chapter to focus the next
  exercise.

The group needs support to make order out of all the thinking and praying. Allow the conversation to guide an order that mixes the genres from visual to music to word. Guide them into an order that will work in your church, even though it will have a particularly energetic feel on this occasion. Allocate roles for Sunday and check who needs support before then.

Prayer

Return to the prayers written on the cards. As you hold them again, add more prayer to the original.

End with a prayer by one of the leaders and the Grace.

Taking leave of one another

- Arrange how the prayer cards will be placed on the altar on Sunday.
- Agree on the venue for the next session.
- Check who will read and pray on the theme of peace.
- Ask people to look out for newspaper articles about conflict or reconciliation in the world or your neighbourhood in the coming days and bring them to the next occasion.
- Who will provide refreshments or will they be offered by your host?

6 Sharing Christ's Peace

Facing God and neighbour to end fear and be part of creation's transformation

Over recent years church communities have mostly restored the sharing of Christ's Peace, which was an important sign of unity in the Eucharist of the early Christian centuries. When this was first reintroduced, many people were very wary and some churches definitely 'didn't do the Peace', viewing it as an interference in their personal relating to God. The revival of the Peace is an indicator of just how much the communal dimension in worship now balances the individual.

In practice it usually takes the form of a handshake, though a full embrace or kiss is more natural to close friends and relatives. Although to an observer it may seem to be merely a belated 'Good morning' or 'How are you?' kind of greeting, there are deeper levels to explore.

Sharing in the presence of Christ

The risen Christ came to the frightened disciples hiding in the upper room and brought a peace from God that they otherwise could not have experienced (Luke 24.36–43). The eucharistic life can bring a deep peace to those who, over years, grow more fully into participation. It's a sign of the peace that uniquely Christ brings to remove conflict in relationships and communities.

The act of sharing the Peace says that it's only because we are one in Christ, daring to offer our deepest loyalty to him, that such an amazingly unlikely bunch of people, with a tendency to be in disagreement, can belong together. Yet if we are honest, competition and suspicion still prevents churches – globally and locally – from having the humility to work as one. Despite God's gift of peace, our authenticity as a eucharistic community is in doubt when in our own life we cannot find equality, justice and mutuality.

At a Eucharist that focuses on reconciling and healing, the laying on of hands and anointing with oil can be a bodily reminder of Jesus' presence with us in our pains and anguish and offering a deep sense of God's release and forgiveness (Mark 5.23–34). We are taken back to the truth that joy and thankfulness flow from knowing that our sins are forgiven and memories healed (Matt. 26.6–13).

Committing ourselves to working for shalom

Shalom is a Hebrew word for which 'peace' is a very inadequate translation. It must include the justice or completeness that come uniquely from sharing in God's life the source of all final peace. Sharing the Peace is more than a handshake or a hug to share a sentimental feeling of goodwill. Yes it is joyful and humanly engaging, but it carries a prophetic edge. Here we are pledging ourselves once more, with all our limitations, to be part of Christ's resistance movement towards violence and all that stands in the way of the coming kingdom.

Jesus' preaching and healing message was about the reign of God that came near through his ministry. This was the theme of many parables and miracles (Matt. 13; Luke 10.25–37). Jesus named and cast out the forces that were opposing God's purposes (Mark 5.1–20). He was not presenting a kingdom that many would have preferred – based on keeping ethical rules, keeping separate from the world or eliminating the Romans. Sharing the Peace subverts such longings in our own day. Now see Figure 7 (overleaf).

The kingdom, says Jesus, doesn't come just where you would expect (Matt. 24). You get glimpses of it wherever you find reconciliation, a huge debt is forgiven, someone hears a cry for justice, someone goes beyond the call of duty, gives a cup of water to or visits a prisoner or feeds the hungry (Matt. 25.31–end; John 4.34).

66 As God wants to live in solidarity with us, so we are called to do the same for others. This solidarity extends to all of creation . . . the transformation of everythng God has created. 99
(MARGARET LAVIN)

Figure 7: Working with God for a good end

So sharing the Peace is also an acted prayer: that we shall be connected to all in heaven and earth who desire the kingdom; and that despite all appearances, such a miracle may occur (Ezek. 11.19; Luke 10.27).

The Church as initiator of another way

So to 'do church' is to be a sign or sacrament of the alternative 'communion' way of the kingdom, as:

- an open and outward-moving community;
- a worldwide Church that walks with all in need;
- a local eucharistic community turned inside out to serve neighbourhood needs.

The life of the Church and its everyday tasks should be joyful. There are many changes required today of those who serve the Church's ordained ministry. There never was a greater need for spiritual maturity in the search for collaborative ways of working. There can be stresses as those who prefer working alone learn how to share responsibility in teams and explore how to be both friend and servant in public ministry (John 13).

In recent years we have learnt again that not only ordained and licensed ministers, but all have vocations. Inevitably, to get the point we have often so overemphasized the role of all God's people that the representative and overseeing tasks of the ordained have been overshadowed. If we believe that all Christians make distinctive contributions to God's mission through the Church and beyond, we must clarify the focus and relation between particular ministries – deacon, priest, Reader ministry team or lay minister. This is an urgent task both to model to society how unity is comprised of difference, and to free up local churches from introspection for their tasks of mission and evangelization.

The New Testament also dismantles any idea of church as a pyramid with a few important people telling everyone else how things should be. We should understand the notion of *episkope* (from which we get 'bishop'), not as a private top-down power but as, organically, the corporate oversight of the whole Church.

> 66 We need conversion because we are always holding something back, because there will always be more room in our hearts for love. 99
>
> (DENNIS JOSEPH BILLY)

> 66 If the church is to be in any sense an exemplary community, a community that demonstrates the possibilities and the blessings of loving fellowship, it must take very seriously in its own life the message and the principles it offers to the world. 99
>
> (DUNCAN B. FORRESTER)

> 66 Mutual ministry is not about assigning people jobs, it is about helping members of communities become aware of who they are as God's beloved. 99
>
> (KEVIN L. THEW FORRESTER)

> 66 Community makes present the 'life-giving power' of God in the midst of 'death-dealing powers' of oppression and dehumanization, to establish 'an alternative world of justice and well being'. 99
>
> (KATHLEEN McALPIN, quoting ELISABETH SCHÜSSLER FIORENZA)

This is the way to understand 'communion', as a kaleidoscope of different Christians supporting one another as disciples and ministers.

Notes for leaders: Session 6

Sharing Christ's peace

Gently does it

After the intercessions the congregation stands to share the Peace of Christ with one another. This is often introduced with a scriptural verse or phrase to highlight the theme of the day.

Preparation: what needs to be planned in advance

This journey is about everyone being on this bus, not two drivers and twelve passengers. Going out allows one-to-one conversations as you travel. These often have amazing results as we learn from one another.

What readings will be needed and how will they be available if you are visiting another place or building?

The meeting place will have been agreed some while ago and now needs to be finally checked.

As the session will have a fixed date, being flexible within different possibilities – depending on the weather – is vital and good learning.

Setting up the session

The point of the meeting is to go deeper into what it could mean to share the Peace of Christ. The session needs to start together in some 'gathered space': it can be the church, someone's home or at the place you're visiting. Explain about God's peace to your host or visitor, depending on what you've arranged. Just let it flow and be guests.

The session in action

Lighting a candle

Wherever we are we have been able, so far, to light a candle to alert us to God's unfailing presence. Find a way to do this wherever you are going (providing your host agrees and it is safe). Otherwise use your imagination to show how Christ is among you in this session. For this exercise, see if you can manage to carry a number of small candles or tea lights (with holders) and a box of matches or lighter. Perhaps you could take a small gift from your church to leave for your host.

Introducing the theme

Leaders first check if there are comments from the last session. Ensure these are carefully heard.

Introduce a few of the strands from the chapter such as that only Christ's Peace is capable of holding together such a diverse group of people in one community. Look at how different you all are in this group as well as in the church community as a whole.

Is that true of the parish where your church is set?

What is peace? Let members describe to the group the conditions in which you actually find peace or where you imagine finding peace:

- Who would be with you?
- Where would you be?
- Would there be music or silence?
- Would you be outside or indoors?

Let the group ask more questions and suggest which other sentences or ideas in the chapter connect with them.

Readings

Let Scripture, poems or sentences from the chapter be read. Wherever you're meeting, see what there is around the place that speaks of peace or its absence. Have a search to look for notices, images or information. What about newspaper cuttings on conflict or reconciliation that people may have brought?

Some questions for conversation

In sharing the Peace:

- We're dramatically expressing our desire for God's kingdom to come, starting with us.
  What would it mean for God's kingdom to start growing in you or us? Think of specific examples.
- We're saying to one another and to God, 'We will gladly accept the gifts of the Spirit to help us be part of bringing in God's reign.'
  What gifts of the Spirit are you aware of having been given? How are they put to the service of the kingdom?
- We will follow the narrow way, the way of the cross – even though 'before the cock crows, you will deny me three times' (Matt. 26.34).
  What does the narrow way mean? Within the confidentiality of this group,

can we share any ways in which we deny Christ? (Matt. 7.14).

- We're promising, in God's power, to be agents of this kingdom coming, as Jesus taught us in the new shape of praying he gave to the disciples, 'Our Father' (Luke 11.2).
  How are we special agents of God's plans? Read the Lord's Prayer for clues.

- In practice, in our local community we are promising to act with kindness and patience in the Spirit of Christ, especially towards 'the poor' in every sense (Matt. 25).
  When did your church last show 'kindness' or 'patience' to those beyond it?

- It's important that we are realistic about the gifts we have been given. Often we hear this best from others.
  What gifts do group members and leaders see in each other?

Also take time to look at the text of your worship and see just where 'the Peace' comes in the regular order of things.

Discuss experiences of sharing the Peace:

- *What are we sharing?*
- How do we imagine this builds us as a community and as agents in the world?

Prayer

This is a good chance to share Christ's Peace with care, imagination and joy. At the Exodus the Israelites ate the Passover, dressed and standing, ready for the journey (Exod. 12.11–13). Before leaving, stand with your coats on ready to go out. Try to create the feel of a community on the move, as the disciples might have felt as they were sent out by Jesus at Pentecost (Acts 2).

- Include your host in the sharing of the Peace in a circle with the group, and leave a lighted candle (provided they wish it, in both cases).
- Make sure any who are vulnerable are safely delivered home.
- Write on behalf of your group and thank your host.
- You might also add an invitation to the Confirmation service and a phone number.

Taking leave of one another

- Where will you be meeting next time?
- Who will provide refreshments?
- Who will pray and read?

Leaders' reflection

- So how did it go this time?
- Were we well enough prepared?
- Was the physical space supportive of the session?
- What did you learn yourself?
- Think of a question arising out of this experience.

7 Offering Gifts and Preparing a Feast

Giving thanks that we have a place in the mystery of God's love

The Offertory procession

From the second-century account of Justin Martyr we recognize the long tradition of people offering the food of the eucharistic celebration. A core practice is for one or two people from the congregation to approach the altar, carrying bread (or more likely specially made communion wafers), wine and water. At celebrations like Easter Day other gifts of honey, fruit or milk can emphasize the nurturing gifts of Christ for the baptized in the Eucharist. Sometimes individuals and groups will bake the loaf to be offered, blessed, broken and shared.

However this procession happens, it's a reminder that we find ourselves in a round-table partnership that works from the premises that:

- everything in creation comes from and returns to God – we're involved in our challenging task as stewards of the world and its people;
- we're given almost overwhelming gifts – so instead of anxiously calculating life from a sense of deficit and selfishness, we may choose to be creative and thankful (Col. 3.14–21);
- our entire existence, fears and joys are taken up to the altar in the offered bread, wine and money, to

be open to and transformed by God's holiness – this includes everything about us and not just the parts we're happy with and proud of;

- whatever stage of life we're at, whether just setting out or confident adults with tasks and responsibilities and relationships, or whether we've stumbled in some way, been damaged by life or are starting to experience a failing body, ageing mind, dementia and disease – all of these are offered to remind ourselves that 'Jesus is Lord' and that we've given over our lives to be in Christ who is risen;

- when we've emptied our hands through giving over everything, we receive our lives back as a blessing and gift from God.

Offering up our daily work

As Christians at work we may be fired by a saying of Jesus such as, 'just as you did it to one of the least of these who are members of my family, you did it to me' (Matt. 25.40). In the middle of global hunger and ecological disasters and, more locally, financial crises and uncertainty over health care and social services, what can it mean to be offering up our lives in the Eucharist? How do we connect our worship with being a disciple of Christ in the workplace and the intercultural environment that is today's world?

Where is there room in our working life for God when:

- despite the fine holistic speeches of leaders of the multinationals, their chief aim is to create wealth, more prosperous living standards for some and a high yield for investors?
- colleagues steal ideas without giving due credit?
- there's an expectation that, like everyone else, you will act dishonestly?
- institutional racism or sexism is condoned by those in charge?
- promotion depends on being prepared to neglect oneself and family?

Yet managers have begun to realize that focusing only on financial success can be counterproductive and lead to stagnation.

We must learn to discern when there are others who may not be actively disciples but with whom we share a spiritual affinity. Can we listen carefully to discover those who are concerned for ethical choices and justice and with whom we can cooperate to make a difference?

Local church groups should be offering a forum for work issues – see Figure 8.

 **place where we . . .**

 can be opened to faith by meditating on the story of Zacchaeus coming down from his tree

 have courage to ask questions at work about corporate values

 acknowledge that God is the final authority in the world

 see things differently as witnesses to Christ in this world

can be seen as cooperating in God's creative activity

 share dilemmas together

 are attentive to the voice of the Holy Spirit

Figure 8: A forum for work issues

❝ God is one who is
permanently coming to our
bleak, unfinished reality,
filling us with strength
and power until the life of
God-with-us becomes all
in all. ❞

(PHILIP ENDEAN)

Whether our work is running a home, parenting, teaching, gardening or the work that others are not prepared to do, it has the potential to be lived out as a following of Christ. Sometimes, though, it can be very difficult to see the connection with the suggestion that Christ calls us to this.

In offering 'ourselves, our souls and bodies', as Cranmer puts it in the Book of Common Prayer, we have our true selves revealed to us. Despite what society or we ourselves may see, whether we are male or female, child or adult, straight or gay, local or foreign, old or young, fit or enfeebled – when we surrender our lives in the Offertory we become a blessing and a gift for all.

God in all places

Scripture links God's holiness with justice and protest at obstacles placed in the path of the poor. Rather than offering up 'the poor' as 'other people in distress', the Eucharist invites us *all* to be blessed as God's poor. When we ask questions about the causes of poverty we soon bump into racial, cultural and religious prejudices. Poverty is not accidental but a situation brought about by public and social structures and by social greed.

Moses' vision of the burning thorn bush, Jacob's ladder from heaven to earth and Isaiah's anointing of the Lord's servant remind us that it is often in encounter with extreme human situations that God is known. Those who have worked as street pastors, prison or hospice chaplains or taken part in retreats on the streets remind us of the dangers for church communities of avoiding the presence of God among those who are:

- sleeping in derelict property;
- seeking asylum;
- spending the entire day looking for work;
- victims of poverty and other forms of injustice;
- dying of disease, neglect, brutality or starvation;
- victims or perpetrators of violence;
- addicted to pornography;

- drug dealers and users;
- radicalized into terrorism.

Including all human brokenness and our own into the Offertory procession is a first step in churches opening drop-in centres or supporting educational and rehabilitative programmes or challenging the basis of a society with such symptoms of corporate dis-ease.

Offering money

- As God gives Godself generously, so God's people will be identified as giving in a way that is only possible in the power of God (Luke 6).
- We offer gifts to God so that we are transformed into people who give.
- Jesus urged his disciples to love God enough to be able to be detached from their earthly wealth (Luke 12). He challenged the rich and pious young man to sell his possessions for the poor (Luke 18.23).
- The Acts of the Apostles describes the communion of God's people in terms of a complete lifestyle, rather than something fitting into an existing way of seeing things.
- This is illustrated in the radical sharing of possessions and the distribution to those suffering hardship (Acts 2.44–47).

Churches that at one time managed well on invested capital now depend almost entirely on the live giving of congregations to meet local costs and to pay for regional infrastructure, clergy stipends and pensions. Some Anglican churches are proud to be in places they can't afford because other, wealthier churches share their financial resources with less prosperous ones. This is an intentional sign of the communion of all God's people. However, when churches within one international communion refuse to bear with one another's differences, largely created by contextual, cultural and educational forces, they are undermining the Church's vocation to reveal God's nature and purpose as mutual and generously inclusive.

Setting the table

Carefully and simply laid directly on the wood or stone altar top, or on the white linen altar cloth, are:

- a corporal (square white linen cloth) on which stand:
  - vessels (usually made of precious metal or pottery) consisting of:

    a paten – a small round plate to hold a large wafer or piece of bread;

    a chalice – a drinking cup for wine, mixed with a small amount of water;

    a ciborium – a chalice-shaped container with a lid for the bread for the congregation.

66 For as often as you eat this bread and drink the cup, you proclaim the Lord's death until he comes. **99**

(1 COR. 11.26)

66 I will not eat it until it is fulfilled in the kingdom of God. **99**

(LUKE 22.16)

66 Have we begun to glimpse what this might mean for our own living and dying and for the destiny of humanity? **99**

(NICHOLAS PETER HARVEY)

So now we're ready for the Eucharistic Prayer. The Eucharist is the feast of the resurrection. The Last Supper and the meals after the resurrection, such as at Emmaus or by the lakeside, showed God in the face of Jesus. The invited guest at Emmaus becomes the host. Eating with Jesus was and remains a looking towards the final face-to-face relationship with God.

To prepare to break bread and share wine around and from this altar table is, as at the Peace, to be eagerly desiring to be part of the wild hope that God's coming reign will mean for all life. This piece of drama carries the long history of God's presence together with abundance and presence now.

A torn piece of loaf and a mouthful of wine speak dramatically of celebration, communal feasting and of the overwhelming blessings Christ has in store.

Notes for leaders: Session 7

Offering gifts and preparing a feast

Drinking in – praying out

The prayers of the people and the sharing the Peace bring to an end the focus on hearing and responding to God's word, and the Offertory naturally begins the period of focusing on the table or altar. It's common for members of the congregation to present wine, water and bread, together with the collection of money for the work of the church, both locally and more widely. A hymn will often be sung here. As the hymn ends and when the table is laid, the presider will offer a prayer dedicating the gifts and involving the lives of all present as a renewed offering to God's service.

Preparation: what needs to be planned in advance

Leaders, this can be an 'active' session, in church or wherever you can meet to cook. You could also choose to turn water into wine (see below), make scones, bread or 'Pilgrims' Soup' together (everything goes in that you have to hand!).

If you're choosing the various baking and cooking options, what does that imply for venue and equipment and safety issues?

As you plan to make food or drink together, expect to talk about how God is present in ordinary things. How does Scripture remind us of this?

Decisions will need to be made, probably before the course begins, about who can lead this session successfully and what support you may need from outside. This is a good way of involving your own wider church community or someone from a neighbouring church. Make sure you have the ingredients mentioned in the session below and are clear about what will take preparation time.

This session creates friendship, laughter and a bond through working together. You might decide to cook or bake together on more than one occasion, depending on how much time you have. Our experience of this proved to be one of the most meaningful opportunities for sharing. It does need careful advance planning and resourcing. The notes for this session offer you one possible route. By now you may be able to see other possibilities that will work better in your situation.

Resources for the leaders

- Notice how many different forms of table grace we know of.

- Discuss how in different situations the Eucharist in many forms recurs in the Christian Church almost everywhere.

- Consider human life – planting, growing, harvesting, eating, giving thanks and being sustained by God who is Lord of life.

- Almost everyone takes part in eating and drinking. You may want to do some basic research to compare how different religions have different rules, for example Judaism and Islam.

- 'Give us each day our daily bread' in the Lord's Prayer (Luke 11.3) reminds us that the making, selling, providing, eating and sharing of food is a vital sign of all our relations under God.

- In both the Old and New Testaments, God is the clear source of food (Gen. 37; Exod. 16; 1 Kings 17; Matt. 6.11; 14.15–21; Luke 22.14–23; John 6.31, 51; 21.1–14; 1 Cor. 11.23).

Here are just a few of the famous food stories and images found in the Bible:

- Jacob gives Esau stew in exchange for Esau's birthright (Gen. 25.29–34);

- Joseph controls the food supply in Egypt (Gen. 41.46–57);

- God feeds Israel in the desert (Exod. 16.14–18);

- Ruth gleans grain in the field of Boaz (Ruth 2.2–9);

- God prepares a table in the presence of enemies (Ps. 23);

- Satan tempts Jesus (Matt. 4.3–11);

- The wedding banquet at Cana (John 2.1–11);

- Jesus feeds 5,000 (Mark 6.34–44);

- The command to feed the hungry (Matt. 25.35–40);

- The returning son (Luke 15.23–27);

- Parables of sowing, storing grain, banqueting and working in the vineyard (Mark 4.1–12; Luke 12.18–21; Matt. 20.1–16);

- Jesus celebrating a Passover meal (Mark 14.12–25);

- The risen Christ comes to supper at Emmaus (Luke 24.13–32).

The session in action

Light your candle, welcome everyone and share what has happened to people during the week. This might be offered in prayer later.

> To increase the chances of the group growing in *presence* with one another, and if you think it helpful, check again, gently, that everyone has the same view of the confidentiality of the group: you can take away what you learn about God, yourself and how to live well, not what you learn about someone else.

Introducing the theme

Initiate conversations on these themes:

- On page 85 we read that all our lives, fears and joys are carried up to the altar in the offered bread and wine to encounter God's holiness and be transformed. In twos try to work out what this means for you.

- Page 86 suggests that whatever stage of life we're at, it can be offered to remind ourselves that 'Jesus is Lord' and we have given over our lives to be in Christ who is risen. Are there real experiences to connect with here?

- When our hands are empty we can receive our lives back as a blessing and gift from God. Literally, 'blessing' is about being spoken well of. There are many scriptural passages on this theme, such as Samuel being anointed king, prophets appointed by God against their will, Mary's invitation to be the mother of the Christ child or Jesus' experience when baptized by John. Find such narratives in the Bible and, looking again at page 88, ask what it means to see our lives as blessed by God.

This session is about being present to God, not just in the parts of ourselves that we're proud of but in all that we are and all that we have, symbolized in what we bring to the table to be transfigured.

Turning water into wine

- If you're up for this, you'll have to decide who within the leaders and the group is 'in the know' beforehand.

- If you are very fortunate you might find an enthusiastic winemaker to show how it is done.
- A leader works with the 'winemaker'.

Read the account of the wedding at Cana (John 2.1–11). Notice how important that was as the first public sign Jesus offered about the abundant blessings of God, a new way for us be present to God. Reflect on what St John is saying here about Jesus and the overwhelming blessings of the Father. Relate this to our contemporary blessing in community, Scripture and Eucharist.

Make reference also to Jesus' command at the Last Supper for the community to continue gathering around the new covenant of the risen Christ (Luke 22.1–23).

Discuss what is known within the group of winemaking. Consider the need to be thoughtful, skilled, patient, concentrated and orderly. What are the right ingredients? Start with yeast . . . As the use of the ingredients is demonstrated, the winemaker gathers all around the table, which holds a clear glass bowl of water and all the ingredients. This is a time of conversation, anticipation and questions.

Prayer

From here we move to a time of prayer. People settle in a circle around the table. The winemaker starts the prayer time by remembering the need for an extra jug. The helper brings from the kitchen a second ceramic jug with a little red cordial in the bottom. The jug is ceramic and deep with a narrow neck (so the cordial can't be seen). Because this jug is brought to the table after everyone is seated, the cordial is not visible.

Concentrate on asking God to take our ordinariness, which we bring to the table and use for something extraordinary. Encourage people to come to the table one at a time and offer a prayer for a situation or person close to their heart: someone in trouble, a friend in need, places at war, hospitals and so on. As each one offers their prayer they take a scoop of water from the bowl and add it to the jug.

Everyone is encouraged to come to the table and take a little water from the glass bowl and pour it into the jug, with or without words.

This prayer (or your own words) is spoken:

Lord, take the ordinary prayers offered by our group and turn them into something extraordinary – just as you took the water at Cana and turned it into rich wine.

The new wine is now poured from the jug into the glasses and everyone is offered a drink. Done carefully, this looks better than it sounds!

(In developing this activity we gladly acknowledge a debt to John Pritchard, *The Intercessions Handbook*.)

Jesus and food

So we set about making bread, scones and soup. We include the soup because everyone can be involved – chopping, washing or stirring. As the food is cooking, sit down for conversation and learning.

As we wait for the food to cook, we get to the reason for seeing ourselves as poor and in need of spiritual food. We might discuss this and consider the following together: the Eucharist is always a gift; there is no charge for attending, yet we contribute what we believe God's work is worth.

A health check when we decide what to give in the offering of 'alms' or collection could be:

- What's it worth to me?
- What else could I buy with this money that society would tell me, 'I'm worth it'?
- How far do I believe I am part of Christ's risen body working in the world?

Eating together

Before you sample what you have made, introduce the idea of saying a grace or thank you to God before every meal. Share experiences or interest in this.

Make enough bread for the Sunday Eucharist, in fact make more than enough – simply experience God's abundance. Then suggest that people be given larger pieces of bread than usual – and more wine and enough time to consume them reflectively and with enjoyment.

For Sunday, ask if there is a short time in the service to tell the congregation what you have been doing and where the bread comes from. Remind people just who is on this journey and ask for a mention as part of the intercessions.

Taking leave of one another

Prayers are shared – everyone has a line or two to add. You may use a psalm or a hymn said slowly and reflectively, perhaps saying a verse each in turn.

End with the Gloria, said or sung together.

Check plans for the following week, including readings and prayers – you will be on an outdoor walk. Ask people to bring some food or a flask to share if you are away from a built-up area. Alternatively your host may want to offer you refreshments.

> I'm pleased to have everyone in the restaurant after hours and help them on their journey – it feels as if God is at work through this ministry of food.
>
> (Eric Lewis, priest and coffee shop proprietor)

Leaders' reflection

- How did the practicalities work out?
- What would we do differently another time?
- Were there any hazards?
- What was learnt?

8 Do This

Praising, thanking and remembering Jesus
as part of God's wild hope for the world

Life as praise

Once the table is laid, the Eucharistic Prayer begins with an exchange between presider and people. 'The Lord is here.' 'God's Spirit is with us.' We lift our 'hearts', our whole selves to the presence of God. Like balloons filled with helium, when they are not held down our lives naturally go up. So in the eucharistic liturgy we say or sing, 'Holy, Holy, Holy Lord, God of power and might, heaven and earth are full of your glory. Hosanna in the highest' (inspired by Isaiah. 6.3). All the worshippers speak or sing together – in company with 'angels, archangels, and all the company of heaven'. The praise of God's glory is the creative space in which humanity comes to its fullest flowering. In letting ourselves be open, in response to God's overwhelming love, we discover a true sense of who we are.

❝ Eucharist is the practical activity which founds church: 'The Lord's (or Last) Supper' – in which Christians share in the life, death and resurrection of Jesus Christ – is the pure primal event by which righteousness was constituted in Jesus' time, and it is fully recalled each time it is re-enacted. ❞

(DANIEL W. HARDY)

Who we really are

When we see young children securely loved we're reminded that only as we receive love, affirmation and security do we have a sense of our worth and the confidence to continue growing in our character. Churches, through creating an ethos of welcome to the presence of children in public worship, have a great opportunity to demonstrate this truth.

Sharing how God sees the world

God's particular kind of power is shown in Jesus. But as Jesus' crucifixion shows most clearly, radically, God respects our freedom to reject the love we are offered, even when this leads to utter disrespect and to death itself.

Being blessed by God

As the healing of the ten lepers shows, it is those who give thanks who profoundly receive God's blessing (Luke 17.11–19). In Jesus we see, in concentrated form, all that can be meant by 'blessing':

- God blessing people to be free to be their fullest selves (Ps. 28.6–7; 2 Cor. 4.6);
- people blessing God in song, painting, writing and daily living, as part of God's ongoing creation (Luke 24.50–53);
- the whole earth recognized as held within the scope of God's care and activity (Ps. 47.1–9; 50.7–23; Isa. 48.12–13; Phil. 2.9–11).

Becoming more grown up

Habitually praising God, as upholder and inspirer of our lives, even when we feel disinclined, can lift us from despair and tragedy. As we know from the Old Testament, God works impossibilities and wonders. The poem in Micah 4.1–5 tells of God:

- inviting us to think beyond the present situation;
- offering hope for the future;
- assuring us that God's healing purpose will be achieved;
- expecting us, God's people, to be part of that task.

When we weave our praise of God into all the uncertainties and agonies of living, nothing looks the same (1 John 3.2; 2 Cor. 13.6).

Life as thanksgiving

Week by week, over the years, through joining in the prayer around the table, we are formed in the habit of thankfulness. This goes further than a human saying thank you when people give us good things. To see this, let's ask – for what are we giving thanks?

- ☐ for all that has happened in the past;
- ☐ for being part of God's constant presence in the baptizing community;
- ☐ for God who has created us and made us 'good';
- ☐ for being lifted out of self-centredness through being shown how all life is gift;
- ☐ that baptized into God's people, filled with God's Spirit, we are formed and renewed in the Eucharist;
- ☐ for being made who we are, without any work on our part, but only through God's saving presence over centuries;
- ☐ that through seeing our lives as interlinked with God's life, we are transformed;
- ☐ that in *giving* thanks, together, we become the people remade by *giving thanks*.

Life as remembering Jesus

Transformation for Christian communities is linked in the Eucharist with obeying Jesus' command, variously given in the New Testament as to 'take, eat', 'drink', 'take . . . divide' and 'do this'. What features of presence to God are drawn out here?

> ❝ The local eucharistic community is the place where Jesus is remembered, where his presence in communion is celebrated, and where ways are sought and found to participate in the coming reign of God. ❞
>
> (MARTIN WALTON)

Called to share Jesus' death

Remembering a loved one or a past event also makes them present now. Our faith is based on the Lord's active and loving presence. It's more than remembering information about the historic events of Jesus' life and death, but experiencing his presence, now.

Sharing with Christ in his death and resurrection, our horizons open up endlessly. Through letting God be real to us in Jesus, through the Spirit, we now see the world through the eyes of the Trinity. We are no longer passive onlookers but have become agents of creation's completion (Rom. 8.19–24). As Mary responded to the angel's question whether she would allow herself to become the bearer of God's son in the world (Luke 1.38), we are invited to say, 'Yes, I will be part of God's loving purposes; I will allow my life to be shaped; I will be, in my whole life, a channel of God's peace and blessing for others.'

To bear in our bodies the marks of Jesus will be to follow in the self-emptying way of God (Phil. 2.5–11). Jesus' ministry of healing, impossible without his close relationship with the Father (Mark 1.40–42; 5.41; Luke 13.10–13), invites us also to be signs of God's compassion (Phil. 4.8–9).

66 It is another moment out of time brought into time. And they are connected – all these moments, woven together, uniting. As he breaks the bread (at the Emmaus meal) they see again another loaf on another night, broken and shared, and they remember words of dark foreboding – my body, broken, my blood shared. 99

(STEPHEN COTTRELL)

Called to be travelling companions

Words make worlds. Let's move from 'receiving' to 'sharing' Christ's body and blood. How can we be imaginative in our use of space in church? Our sense of being one with Christ and with one another can be enriched by standing together to share communion, maybe in a semi-circle around the altar or in walking meditatively towards the place where bread and wine are being distributed. Experience of this kind is reminding us of our forgiven, confident, joyful selves, poised, like the Israelites standing at the Passover meal, ready to set out on their desert journey, as slaves no longer, but as fellow pilgrims seeking God's Promise (Exod. 12).

Called to receive

In positively sharing in the life of the risen Christ, our inner life with God and relationship with others is deepened. An example of the benefits of being generous and open is when table fellowship is shared. So at a Eucharist that includes a baptism, uniformed organization parade or Remembrance, it's vital to extend a welcome to share bread and wine with all present who are in good standing in their own churches or who perhaps have lapsed for several years. The Eucharist gives us a shape for coping with and living hopefully within whatever life throws at us.

What are the gifts we have received?

For some, our family of origin – parents, brothers, sisters, grandparents – or later our marriage partners, friendships or training in work, will have given us real and practical experience of how to live and relate to others well. For others this may not be true – or we may not see it that way. The eucharistic community can certainly be where such deficits are made up. Here we can be helped to form gospel-shaped habits that enable us to take our place within the plan of God for the world.

Called to be thankful

The world needs the Church to take on its role of helping to make life more human. The Church's faults and mistakes often make this hard to recognize. However, as God sees the world so we, by sharing in the Eucharist, learn to gaze on the world with the same love and compassion. Our giving thanks to God animates our service and friendship of the poor and all who struggle for justice (Mark 3.14; 1 John 2.6).

Notes for leaders: Session 8

Do this

Do this now

This session is about the part of the Eucharist where in sharing bread and the wine we prepare to share Christ with others.

Preparation: what needs to be planned in advance

Suppose in this session you can be mostly outside. Arrange for a morning or afternoon out. Make it a trip to a special place as a way of reflecting on God's presence in ordinary living. Invite someone to be your companion who knows the area well or who regularly walks a dog there, a well-informed twitcher or whoever occupies or owns the land. Be bold and risk being at the mercy of both the elements and the venue.

Last session you asked people to bring some food or a flask to share if you are away from a built-up area. Follow this up.

It is important that all in your group are able to accomplish this outside activity, so choose your venue carefully according to the mobility and fitness of everyone.

The session in action

Lighting a candle

Light it prayerfully at the place where your journey begins. You may start from a home or a sheltered place. It may be a challenge to keep it alight as you walk. There may be other lights – the sun, street lights or the lights in people's homes or around industrial areas. How can these also be reminders of Christ's presence?

Introducing the theme

Choose some passages or images from the chapter to remind everyone on which part of the eucharistic service we are focusing. Have in mind how every celebration of the Eucharist can have an attraction and connection at different moments, for all ages. Is that desirable or possible?

Reflect on the phrase 'for all that has happened in the past' (see page 99), to those who have also been God's people at different moments and in various places. How can the Eucharist help us know our place in a vast network of God's people?

Leaders will explain that the aim of this walk is to look afresh at what we see every day and to be able to observe some of what God has created. Be aware of the topography of the place, of stories about the animals and their owners, of the birds' journey as they cross continents, of all that is going on out there! What human journeys are made here? Why are people and animals making journeys here?

Allow lots of chances for the group to talk and enjoy one another's company. Stop very occasionally to draw people together for something of interest – but only occasionally. Let the walk take up to one hour if possible – but keep an eye out for people who may tire easily.

Looking and listening

Observing your surroundings is a key way of sensing God's presence everywhere. Walk slowly and look closely at things as if preparing to draw or paint them. Stand still and move your eyes and speak out loud in twos for a few minutes what you see – a road, a tree, a barn, machinery, walls and so on. Ask questions, find out what members of the group know about the wildlife or the history of the place where you are. Ask your host about their involvement or work here. Ask what most helps or hinders their work. Ask what they would like to change.

Prayer

Maybe the group have the courage to pray quietly together somewhere outside. Jesus warned us against demonstrating our piety in public, so be relaxed, imaginative, sensitive and bold. The long history of God's people shows that communities grow stronger through witnessing.

Consider:

- Where is God at work in this place here and now?
- What might delight or anger God in this place?
- What connection is there between living thankful lives and being a grown-up or mature Christian community?
- Is there anything we are moved to think about or do differently?

Depending where you are and the time of day, either return to a house, share a very basic picnic or accept hospitality. A shared meal rather than individual picnics develops contact and builds community.

Developing the theme

Reflect on phrases chosen by the group from the chapter, such as: 'for God who has created us and made us "good"'; or 'that baptized into God's people, filled with God's Spirit, we are formed and renewed in the Eucharist'.

Leaders might choose to help the group research references to St Francis and the connections with him now for our relationship with creation. Consider the Franciscan way of life today – in its three orders and prayers and the shape of the cross of St Francis. How do they show us a connection between Christ's presence in the Eucharist and in all living?

What would it mean for us to become people known for our joy and sense of thanksgiving in the whole of life?

You could offer space for the group to hold a conversation with Jesus or the Father, along the lines of:

- What have I done for Christ?
- What am I now doing for Christ?
- What could I be doing for Christ?

Creating a prayer together, here and now, with all you have experienced and learnt together, what would you thank God for?

Have there been on this outdoor experience signs of God's presence or obvious avenues for prayer?

Taking leave of one another

End with a prayer, such as one by St Francis (perhaps adapted from *Joy in All Things: A Franciscan Companion*, Norwich: Canterbury Press, 2002, p. 90) or by Ruth Burgess from *Barefeet and Buttercups*. Or write one of your own. Finally share the following week's venue and plans.

Leaders' reflection

- What worked well?
- What needs still to be learnt and how will that happen?
- Has anyone disappeared and what are we to do about it?
- How is the group doing on 'presence'?
- What effect is it having on the rest of the church community?
- What resources do we need for the next session?

9 Asking the Spirit

*Calling on God's Spirit to make Christ
present and God's future become real now*

Jesus' ministry began in the Jordan with the Spirit
responding to his prayer by descending like a dove
and the voice from haven saying, 'You are my Son, the
Beloved; with you I am well pleased' (Luke 3.21–22).
This shows that humanity's highest desire is to be loved
by God and to please God. To follow Jesus is to:

- let God transform all our desires into wanting the
  kingdom to come;
- be willing, urgently, to be part of its coming (Luke
  9.23–25; 12.29–34; 14.26).

The Old Testament reminds us that asking for something
from God can bring unpredictable results. God's speech
brings things to be. When we dare to pray for the coming
of the Holy Spirit into our lives and to ask the Spirit to
bring the presence of Christ, we really need to *want* our
prayer to be answered. All that we have seen up to this
point in the book comes into play. When we ask for the
coming of the Holy Spirit, we are risking everything.

Nothing will ever be the same again.

What does our church community dare to
become?

Christ's presence among us and in the sacramental
elements is something given from beyond us and
beyond our control. The Holy Spirit is a volatile gift to
the Church at Pentecost. Only the Spirit makes it possible for those early Christians to move on from being

a Jewish renewal movement. It helps them to see, after great searching, that those who are not Jews (Gentiles) can be in Christ without circumcision or keeping food purity laws. The test of whether people and communities are fired by the Spirit lies in who we are becoming and where our hearts truly lie – doing the will of the Father (Matt. 7.21–23).

'Spirituality' is a word that refers to the growth of holiness in communities of disciples. This holiness shows itself in making connections between God's presence in worship and Scripture and God's presence and activity in daily living. Holiness is also present when justice and peace are pursued for the whole of creation, including human relations.

God is the active source of both the fruits and the gifts of the Spirit. In the New Testament we find a catalogue.

The fruits of the Spirit

Love, joy, patience, kindness, goodness, fidelity, gentleness and self-control (Gal. 5.22). These are more intimate or personal than the gifts that are given to us for the general good (1 John 4.1).

The gifts of the Spirit

In Romans 12.3–8 we find a meditation on these. Wisdom, putting the deepest knowledge into speech, faith, gifts of healing, miraculous powers, prophecy, the ability to distinguish true spirits from false, the gift of tongues of various kinds, and the ability to interpret them (1 Cor. 12.4–11).

Broken and shared

The 'fraction', the breaking of the bread after the communal saying of the Lord's Prayer, is a reminder that:

- in the sharing of bread our broken self is transfigured within the true self of God;
- when the Christian community dies to its isolation (as a grain of wheat) it can at last become a loaf of bread, broken for the world (John 12.24).

The Spirit brings dissatisfaction with our performance and the urge to change. The old ways of being church have to die for an emerging Church to be true to God's call and to be able to communicate the broken-body love of Jesus. The call of bishops and clergy or parish and religious communities is to be worked examples of good news (Rom. 6.4).

In our day the changes that are called for in churches and ministers if we are to reflect the mutual and out-flowing love of God include, primarily, being transformed into a deeper maturity – see Figure 9.

In the New Testament, Jesus' followers are slow to learn to stop trying to be top (Mark 9.30–37; 10.31–33). All in the church who are ministers must learn to share authority, to hear honest differences of opinion and, without being defensive, criticism. They must be seeking to relate to the wide range of groups in the neighbourhood and congregation, and be a broker for their mutual learning. They must be glad to welcome the competence of others, to have the intuition to help the community discover consensus. To be leaders they need the vulnerability of being colleagues too. A church on the way towards becoming collaborative in character will be:

- asking questions about the messages we are sending out, intentionally or not;
- self-aware of when our practice is becoming unhealthy or top-down;
- replacing a spirit of competition with one of co-operation;
- recognizing when our habits are no different from those of the local culture;
- becoming 'one of another' (Rom. 12.5) as the basis on which we live and work.

Which of these issues needs most attention for us and our church at this time? What are the next steps? What kind of conversations will most assist the journey?

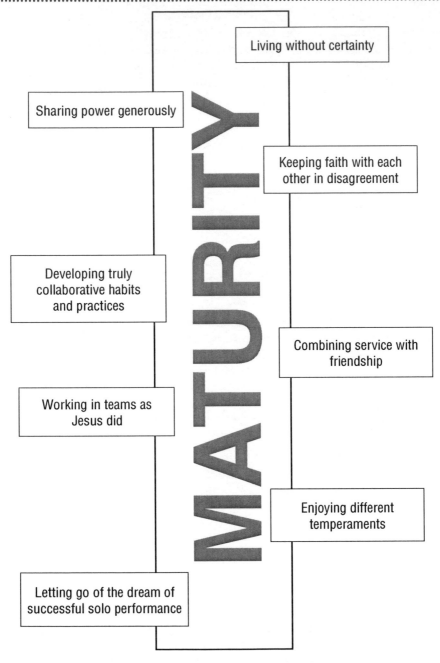

Figure 9: Being a grown-up church

Eat and drink

Eating and drinking at Christ's table is a sign of God's including all people and all creation in salvation. There are other vivid Christian pictures of this truth:

- Jesus opening his arms for us on the cross;
- the Father running towards his returning son and embracing him;
- the way we know God in Jesus as mutual, self-giving Trinity.

Jesus lived in a culture where shared eating was an important sign of welcome, belonging, searching for truth together and being as one. Sharing in God's gift of food with others, even the same dish (Mark 14.20), was both symbolic and a real discovery of companionship. Eucharistic eating and drinking derives from those joyful Jewish table meals that Jesus and his followers shared (Mark 3.18–19). These meals were sometimes with friends (John 12.1–8), with religious leaders (Luke 7.36–50) or with those pushed out of acceptance by society (Mark 2.16; Luke 7.34).

Jesus also hosted outdoor meals of bread and fish for huge crowds, to show how they and the whole world could be healed. Deliberately, he invited them to see these occasions as advance signs of the great heavenly banquet, when God's will for all creation would be completed (Mark 6.30–44). So on the night of his arrest it was natural for him to pour all the intensity of that time into a meal with his closest followers, including Judas who would betray him (Matt. 26.20–30).

Although women are not mentioned here by name, they are recorded as having followed him and served him as part of his ministry team (Mark 15.40–41). They knew that being part of Jesus' self-giving life brings joy, healing and also terror. They showed their gritty discipleship in the face of danger by watching at the foot of the cross.

Here is a test against which to judge our practice of Christianity together. The one thing Jesus insisted must

❝ But as for you, return to your God, hold fast to love and justice, and wait continually for your God. ❞

(HOSEA 12.6)

❝ Hate evil and love good, and establish justice in the gate . . . let justice roll down like waters, and righteousness like an ever-flowing stream. ❞

(AMOS 5.15, 24)

❝ A shoot shall come out from the stock of Jesse . . . The Spirit of the LORD shall rest on him . . . His delight shall be in the fear of the LORD. ❞

(ISAIAH 11.1–9)

be excluded is exclusion itself. If Jesus included all his disciples in all their confusion, and even the one who would be the instrument of his arrest in the Garden of Gethsemane, how would we dare to exclude from our company those:

☐ with whom we disagree;

☐ who constantly argue with or irritate us;

☐ who take us to court;

☐ of different churches;

☐ with different educational background;

☐ of a different race or gender;

☐ who are seeking asylum;

☐ at a different stage of life from ourselves;

☐ who have committed crimes;

☐ whose lives seem shocking to us;

☐ who vote for other political parties;

☐ of different sexual orientation;

☐ with mental instability;

☐ who have disabilities;

☐ who are wealthier or poorer;

☐ who have never learnt how to love.

Jesus gave his message in wonderful deeds of healing, forgiveness and inclusion. He showed us what it's like to be part of a new 'covenant'.

Making truth real

There has been a long tradition of the presider and ministers receiving the bread and wine first, as head of a hierarchy. Again, approaching a 'high' altar to kneel with head bowed has been a way of sensing and humbly receiving the awesome mystery and the wonder of God's reconciling presence (Isa. 6). No single metaphor or physical act will capture the entire meaning of the Eucharist. Different generations of insight will bring new possibilities.

The narrative of Exodus 12 inspires some to recognize, in standing to receive the bread and wine, a vital image of a missionary community. The liberation of a slave people began as they stood, poised for a journey, their eyes set on God's promised hope.

As a counter to our consumer society, how might God's baptized people share communion rather than take or receive within a clerical top-down structure? Among the baptized and baptizing community:

- intimacy, friendship, suffering and mutuality, together with God's hiddenness, beauty and utter closeness, can be revealed around a nave altar – space, voice inflection, gesture, silence, lighting and music can all contribute to the ambiguity of our experiencing the Holy;

- young ones will have a chance to sit at the front to see how the Eucharist is prepared and offered;

- young ones will have been prepared to receive communion before Confirmation;

- those with mobility problems receive first, in their places;

- the congregation move to stand at places where the bread and cup are offered;

- there is no sense of hurry as people wait in a reflective mood, bow, stand or make the sign of the cross;

- songs that reach the heart of faith are played and sung quietly;

- parents carry young children, ministers go on one knee to bless the small ones;

- frequent eye contact is made between people and minister, who knows much of what they are having to bear and are rejoicing in;

- ministers share communion together, the celebrant last;

- a corporate silence is held before we speak and sing words of thanks and celebration.

Notes for leaders: Session 9

Asking the Spirit

Holy smoke

In the course of the Eucharistic Prayer, the Great Thanksgiving, the presider calls on the Holy Spirit to make Christ present among God's people and in the bread and wine on the altar.

Preparation: what needs to be planned in advance

Again, you will need to plan which parts of the material in the chapter to focus on – Sue here just offers one pathway among many.

This session works well in the church where you regularly worship. It usually turns out that most people's awareness of the detail of the space, especially unfamiliar corners, is very sketchy. Today, through exploring and noticing in slow motion, it can become more familiar, so that the group develops a stronger sense of being 'at home'. At the same time, though, the opposite will also become true.

The more we are present to God the more we realize that in God's house, radically, all are guests and no one must ever lapse into considering themselves the host.

The leaders need to meet 15 minutes before the group begins, specifically to pray expectantly for the Holy Spirit to work within the gathering and within each person.

The session in action

Lighting a candle

This time ask someone to place it on the altar while another reads Psalm 122 – one of the psalms of ascent from the days of Israel's temple worship.

Take a moment to check how everyone's week has been. Ask each person to say just a few sentences about what has occupied them this week or any thoughts about the last session.

Introducing the theme

We are focusing today on the work of the Holy Spirit to make us a community to serve God's activity in all life.

Together, pick out some sentences from the chapter and use them to create conversation.

In this session we try to get to know our place of worship as an intense place, crucible or theatre where, if we are present, God's Spirit ignites us. If we are to be part of a community, open to the Spirit who gives us gifts for the world's well-being, we need to be familiar with its everyday objects and symbols and reflect on their deeper symbolism.

In this session the 'tone' changes, part-way through, from activity to an expectant stillness.

Activity A

This will depend very much on the approach your church has to symbolism and the material as a sign of God's presence. If this session as presented wouldn't work for you, be creative and consider why not, and also imagine, positively, what would work better.

Ask a churchwarden, sacristan or server, or whoever takes charge of the space in your place of worship, to show you the liturgical vestments and the special places within the building, such as the font and the lectern. Try not to get too hooked into historical accounts, though that is a vital part of remembering God's Spirit working in every generation. Consider instead how these things can speak to us now. But perhaps they've lost their original ability to help us. What would we want to put in their place?

Let people handle the vestments or try them on if they wish. Explore together how the colours of the stoles and chasubles highlight the theme of particular seasons, for example Advent, Lent or Easter.

It may help to make a 'liturgical clock' showing the number of weeks in each season throughout the year.

Explore the aumbry, the vestry, or the organ or other musical instruments.

Consider why some churches keep the sacrament 'reserved' with an associated white light – partly for the benefit of those who need to receive communion in their homes and partly to know Christ's presence in prayer and in every part of living.

Explain the font and the importance of water and baptism. Make this tour significant by allowing young people in particular to poke about and ask questions. Leave no stone unturned – especially the vessels in the safe or vestry used for the Eucharist.

Activity B

Refer back to the setting of the table for the Eucharistic Prayer (page 90) and relate this to calling the Holy Spirit to make Christ present in the bread and wine and in our community and individual lives.

Preparing candidates for Confirmation means that they need to understand the practicalities, the meaning and the promises. To create an air of expectancy is what you are about to do. Explain and demonstrate what will happen at their Confirmation service according to your tradition. Let each person get a feel for the chalice, taste the wafers – see how you prepare and clear away.

Plan the prayers together for the service, choose hymns and songs, produce a service-sheet cover with your photographs – take ownership of the practical elements of this celebration where you are able. If your tradition is to have Confirmation sponsors then arrange to see them in advance. Make all the preparations you can. Take your refreshments while you do this planning.

When you've finished, change the way the group is gathered by moving into a circle. Settle comfortably. If possible change the lighting to create a more contemplative atmosphere and space. Expect miracles.

Explore how we might expect the Holy Spirit and more of ourselves. What does the chapter say to you about the connection between spirituality, holiness and daily living and the life of our society and world? What would you want to add?

Readings

> By contrast, the fruit of the Spirit is love, joy, peace, patience, kindness, generosity, faithfulness, gentleness, and self-control.
>
> (Galatians 5.22–23)

> Beloved, do not believe every spirit, but test the spirits to see whether they are from God; for many false prophets have gone out into the world.
>
> (1 John 4.1)

At some other time read also 1 Corinthians 12 and Luke 21.

Explore gently the following questions in twos or threes, depending on your group (perhaps have them printed on a card for people to take away and prepare prayerfully for their Confirmation):

- What is it like for me/us to be a disciple/disciples?
- What is it costing me/us?
- What gifts has God given me/us?
- How are they put to work at present?

Ask each person to find a space and write a short prayer for the rest of the group. Gather these in at the end of the session. You may wish to present these again to each member of the group at Confirmation – copy them or scan them into your computer or find a way to create something as a keepsake and reminder of this time together.

Taking leave of one another

End with a prayer spoken by a leader and the Grace.

The next session will be the last planned. There needs to be some conversation around whether there's a future for this group. Individuals could meet with leaders to explore where God has been taking you and how to address any emerging issues or sense of calling.

10   Being Dismissed

*Going out to join earth's future to the
life of heaven*

We come to church to be sent away. After the congregation has shared the bread and wine or received a blessing, the presider holds a reflective silence in which all
ages together can learn to share. We have received and
shared the presence of God in gathering, reconciliation,
the word of Scripture, concern for the world, entering
into a peace beyond our own making, the taking, blessing, breaking of bread and sharing of bread and wine.
What focus does this give to my life and the life of our
community this week?

A prayer of thanksgiving is followed by a final hymn
of celebration. The congregation receives God's blessing
and is sent out to ordinary living, 'to love and serve the
Lord', and they reply, 'Amen'. Music provides a time
for people to move from a spirit of worship to one of
mutual friendship and over refreshments a chance to
catch up with news and share plans for future events in
the community.

Overflowing with God's gifts

As the presider pronounces God's blessing we may carefully retrace the sign of the cross on our own bodies.
Here is the physical recognition that we have been
given amazing quantities of God's forgiveness, wisdom,
reassurance, love, beauty, joy, encouragement and sus-
tenance for the journey.

The image comes to mind of many gallons of good
wine, turned from water, that Jesus freely gave to a

wedding banquet as a sign of God's abundance (John 2.1–11). Our baptismal relationship with God and with one another has been restored. We are assured of our equality in the faith and given power to carry out all that is our unique responsibility in the days ahead.

There's a tendency for us to fit a bit of Christianity into our already busy lives. Just as we eat up all that is God in the Eucharist, so we are to allow God to eat up all that is us. This may seem shocking but it's a reminder that we are not solitary customers in a restaurant or consumers for our own benefit or on our terms. The self-giving love that Jesus shows calls us to be totally open to God, consumed by God and by all God gives us to love.

Go in peace to love and serve the Lord

So we agree to be sent out 'in the name of Christ', as God's people, in all the streets and byways of daily living. We have experienced God's action upon us and now are charged to find out where God is active in the places where we go, and to take our part. But we don't go alone. We take with us the spirit of the eucharistic assembly – the reassurance, the urgency, the peace and the love of Christ. When we depart, the Eucharist goes with us. We go as those who know we are 'God's beloved' within whose hearts the Holy Spirit burns as Jesus speaks to us on the road (Luke 24.32).

What mission?

Recent years have proved a disquieting time to be involved in mission in Western Europe. Many are rightly suspicious of Christian mission. In every era of history we can see often manipulative and abusive practices that could never be true vehicles for the gospel of Jesus Christ. Powerful intellects have been persuasive that Christianity is at best a spent force and at worst a serious block to human maturing. Christian faith always comes packaged in particular times and places, intertwined in one culture or another.

The kind of relationships that churches foster –

between children and adults, women and men, young and old – need to be of a piece with the gospel. It's easy for 'weak' churches to look with envy at churches experiencing great 'success'. Charismatic and Pentecostal churches are growing among those who seek a faith that is demanding, all-embracing and obviously changes lives. The most vibrant Christian communities are in the Global South, the former 'mission field'. Yet this region is the area that poses most challenges for women, be it the raging epidemic of HIV/AIDS, women-trafficking, violence against women, cultural practices oppressive to women, illiteracy, patriarchal structures, male-centric worldviews.

What are the implications and tasks for Christian mission in such context? The so-called historic or mainline churches need to discern what can be learnt from those experiences as we sidestep worn-out habits of church and understandings of how different churches, working together, now approach mission and evangelism.

The Old Testament is clear that being 'in exile' is a situation to be accepted in humility and penitence, rather than with justifications and blame or in a spirit of defensiveness. Exile may initially create a sense of grief but this can turn through reflection into a determination to rediscover and follow God's will. Churches in Europe are largely in exile, the myth of secularism still holding sway.

It could become a healing time if we accept the situation as it is rather than denying it with false pride. Using head and heart, churches need to mourn our failings, listen to people's new search for hope and meaning, and respond creatively. To support this spirit, even when the situation seems dark, we need to remain faithful to eucharistic thankful living and be always turning outwards to the kingdom agenda. 'Rejoice in the Lord always' (Phil. 4.4).

66 The attitudes that should be present in the church in this state of exile today are best summed up in the Beatitudes and in the letter sent to the exiles by Jeremiah (Matt. 5.3–12; Jer. 29.1–23). **99**

(PATRICK WHITWORTH)

What the Church has learnt about mission in recent years

- When we claim to be on a mission we need to recall that it's God's mission in which the Church shares.

Sea changes in the global Christian landscape help us to recognize how radically our understanding of mission has changed in recent times. Fifty years ago, 'mission' still meant evangelism, teaching, nursing and pastoral care, by others, elsewhere. Organized overseas mission work began in earnest in the seventeenth century with the gradual realization of the scale of the rest of the world's population, in the light of Jesus' command to preach the gospel to all nations (Luke 24.47). Over the years many agencies were formed, reflecting the different traditions within the Church. This was a period of sending and giving. Missionaries were trained and sent from Western European Churches, and congregations and individuals gave very generously. The height of this era was the second half of the nineteenth century into the early part of the twentieth. In 1910 the International Missionary Conference in Edinburgh spoke of 'the evangelization of the world in this generation'.

So always the big picture is the mission *of* God (John 3.16–21; 1 John 4.10, 14).

- John 17.18 makes it clear that any mission we have is a sharing in the commission given to the disciples in the new energy of the resurrection.

- Christ's work is unique but those who through baptism are 'in Christ' can be co-workers (John 14.12–14).

- The Holy Spirit given to followers of Christ empowers and gives gifts for sharing in God's mission (John 20.19–23).

- The very nature of the Church is to be commissioned to share in the mission of Father, Son and Spirit (John 14.26).

- The Church in mission stands on the shoulders of Jewish ancestors of faith sought out, and frequently failing, to be God's people over many centuries before Christ.

- Mission, long before the birth of the Church, has been to share with the Trinitarian God in the reconciling and perfecting of the whole creation.

- Church community therefore exists not for itself but always intending to be a proclamation of the patterns of relating that are uniquely the gifts of God and illustrated perfectly in the life of Jesus Christ.

> There has been a long Jewish/Christian tradition of contrasting two cities, Jerusalem and Babylon. The prophet Jeremiah tells God's people of his day that they are in exile in Babylon because they have failed to be faithful witnesses to God. However, all is not lost: they must settle among a strange people, build houses, get married to local people and 'seek the welfare of the city where I have sent you into exile, and pray to the LORD on its behalf, for in its welfare you will find your welfare' (Jer. 29.4–7).

Early Christians saw the Roman Empire as the equivalent of Babylon, a strange, sinful and evil place directed away from the love of God but one in which Christians, for the time being, are called to serve God and share its peace. Although pagan, it can serve the purpose of God, and the wheat and tares can grow together until the harvest (Matt. 13.24–30, 36–43).

As God's people in Britain today we are in exile, but treated largely to apathy rather than aggression. There is a complexity, in that local churches often make hugely significant contributions to neighbourhood life, so long as they don't bother people too much with belief. The Church's faith as such is mistrusted and avoided; we have failed to bear witness in ways that are authentic or connect with most people. But God calls us to live here and for the time being serve the welfare of all the people among whom we live until the return of Christ at the final judgement, the Parousia, when God in Christ through the Spirit will be fully present to all creation.

❝ See, the home of God is among mortals. He will dwell with them; they will be his peoples, and God himself will be with them. ❞

(REVELATION 21.3)

Until then the people of God are fully part of the world.

As Christ comes in judgement, revelation and victory, the true Church, the New Jerusalem, will be separated from Babylon as a bride adorned for her husband (Rev. 21.2). So although God is patient, he wants everyone to respond to his love in the risen Christ. The Church is not waiting quietly and patiently for the end to come but is active and responsible for making Christ known in every place and to every person.

So now God's people are called to do three things at once: to integrate with all the people with whom we share this world, to seek every opportunity to bring hope, forgiveness, care, justice, peace, partnership, the basis of a healthy common life; and to contribute actively to framing a society where all are neighbours – in the sense that the Good Samaritan put aside all his immediate personal matters to rescue a foreigner who would normally have despised him.

Fair Trade or supporting asylum seekers are clearly examples of Christians working for the welfare of the city in which we are set, in partnership with all of goodwill. We are to be makers of hospitality, improvising with all others: to create a society that wants the good of all; to contribute to the welfare of the city in which we are in exile; but third, to have a different horizon, knowing in the end to whom we belong.

We are to invite whoever we can to share our belief and practice of community focused on Jesus Christ, who will, one day, bring all things and peoples to a fuller love and a deeper neighbourliness. However gloomy things may look now, and however we can make a difference, God the Father, who has raised Jesus from the dead, will outdistance all our provisional attempts at goodness.

Sharing in God's mission invites us to become a people that faithfully witnesses, now, to God's final work of perfecting the world. Until then we are to be co-workers for a public and common life that radically treats everyone as a neighbour and contradicts all that treats some as irrelevant or dispensable. As aliens in a foreign land we are to worship and to seek the common good as faithful witnesses to God's coming kingdom, which is Jesus' way of talking about the perfect love that comes when,

> ❝ The Christian acts within a present and a future opened up by Christ . . . It is the Spirit of the risen Christ who announces both the kingdom come and the kingdom yet to come. The church participates . . . by establishing and performing the kingdom come and yet to come. ❞
>
> (GRAHAM WARD)

66 When the church engages the world, she is called to act like salt and get dissolved in it . . . I sense an obvious lack of courage and commitment on the part of the global church to address issues of global justice (social, economic and ecological justice) and religious pluralism and its specific challenges as fundamental mission concerns. 99

(GEEVARGHESE MOR COORILOS)

finally, God has God's way fully with all creation, starting with ourselves. In this time, urgently, God's people must set aside time for praying, worshipping each week, reading Scripture and spending some time in silence in order to be available to God who comes to pitch his tent among us.

In recent decades Churches have begun to act on the recognition that God uses other agencies to transform the world according to the values of the coming kingdom. They have increasingly entered into partnership with one another, with those of other faiths and with secular agencies. It remains a challenge how to hold together the gospel mandate for helping others turn to God in a personal relationship and striving, with others, for social justice and asking prophetic questions about the way the world is ordered.

Eucharistically shaped mission

If we follow the spirit and logic of the previous parts of this book, what shape of mission emerges? It is one of mutuality and self-giving in which all are at first recipients of God's overwhelming blessings in the hope that we shall also become agents of mission to others and they in their turn to yet still others. It has a compelling mandate to expect personal transformation and also a daring challenge to confront, prophetically, global forces of evil.

How we learn from the Global South, where people have lived in multifaith contexts, will be vital. It means stretching our hearts and minds to find what is common among religions, how factors of context, secularization and postmodernity affect our witness, and how we can engage with other faiths and be grounded deeply in our own faith.

If we return to the shape of the eucharistic liturgy with which we began and are now very familiar, how does it shape our living as community and as individual disciples? Through all its aspects, we have seen how the Eucharist as a whole is filled with Christ's real presence; it fires God's people to perform the shape of living in the world that is the early sign of the world finally reconciled in Christ (Eph. 1). A constant theme in these chapters has been the invitation for Christian communities – always in connection with all other communities – to be worked examples of the solidarity that God desires and creates within all creation. All human suffering, brokenness, yearning, joy and fulfilment are underpinned by God's love and unlimited possibilities for goodness and the work of the Spirit.

The Eucharist teaches us that just as Jesus always ministered among his disciples, the good news is known and practised in relationships. Disciples are on pilgrimage together, sharing in *presence*, the never-ending depths of communion. The living communion with God and with one another helps create that final communion of all peoples in creation that is God's passionate desire. 'March towards the splendour. Your God goes with you' (from a wall in the monastery of Lluc, Majorca).

Notes for leaders: Session 10

Being dismissed

Onward and upward

Now the Eucharist ends as we are dismissed to go out with love and peace to serve God's purposes in the world, as agents of God's kingdom.

Preparation: what needs to be planned in advance

This session needs a strong feel of a celebration about it, with really good refreshments. You need a special cake or whatever is a treat to share.

Start the session a bit earlier so that the leaders can meet. Allow an hour for the group to be together and invite visitors to come after that time.

For the second part of your last meeting you might invite session leaders, all who have helped on your journey, family and sponsors to come and help you celebrate. Your parish priest needs to be here for this part of the session and given a role so he or she is not just 'a visitor'. Remember there are no passive observers in conversations that matter.

Make sure someone will have a camera. You might want to take some photographs and use these, and others you may have taken before, to tell the story of your journey and put on the cover of a special Confirmation service-sheet – and/or a poster for the church or the church website, along with a few comments on the experiences of your group.

For the second part of the session you need to give careful thought to a basic structure for the worship into which everyone can put their contribution through music, Scripture, poetry, prayers (which could be spontaneous or from books). It could include a thank you and affirming comment given to each one by each one – spoken or possibly more easily written. Do this before you share refreshments.

For the first part of the session plan how to make sure everyone knows the shape of the liturgy. Consider the possibility of a game as described below.

If you decide on the poster or banner idea (below), what equipment will you need and how will you check with the priest or community how you can display it? What about your parish website for a few short accounts of people's experiences on this course?

Another possibility would be for the group to invite their priest and others to be part of this final worship – it could be a short and simple Eucharist, night prayer or something from the many available resource books. This could be fed over into the Sunday worship.

Afterwards, gather the best of your course comments and photographs. Ask someone with the skill to use them creatively to make a card; give one to each person in the group as soon as possible as a reminder of this journey together.

What will be the final prayer and will your church leaders prepare this?

The session in action

This session leads into a celebration of the work the group has done together. We begin, however, with just the group and its leaders gathering for the last time, inviting others to join later.

Lighting a candle

The final session starts with lighting the candle and prayer offered by one or all of the group spontaneously. It is essentially a celebration, but first of all take some time to review what has been learnt.

Each leader could prompt group reflection on the sessions, in order, refreshing memories, making links and enjoying the achievement. Do this conversationally and address any presenting questions and misunderstandings. Write or draw boldly on a large sheet of paper so all can see it.

A leader helps everyone explore the theme

Emphasize that the bread and wine aspects of the Eucharist are not simply tacked on to the service of the word. Look back at the chapter heads and at a copy of your usual service booklet to be reminded of the 'spine' of the Eucharist from start to finish. Maybe play a game where everyone represents part of the service and stands in line or in a circle to tell everyone which bit they are and how they fit with the others.

In the chapter, what does 'We come to church to be sent away' mean? Or try asking if 'No such thing as a free lunch!' relates to the Eucharist.

What focus does this give to my life and the life of our community from today onwards?

- Which words or quotations from the chapter stand out for you?
- How do you think you might need to respond differently now?

The leaders share what the Eucharist, faith and church community mean for them, and others may be moved to say a few words too.

Celebration

The second part of this session is our celebration.

A short service brings group and visitors together, offering insights for others into the reality of the journey of which your group has been a part.

Refreshments are then shared and photographs taken of the group. As everyone tucks in you can hold a conversation on the subject of the future: everyone's hopes and intentions for a future here as a disciple and perhaps a minister within and for God's people.

Use other passages from the chapter to stretch the conversation further. What is the task of our community in this neighbourhood now? What is your calling already or in the future?

- Talk about projects running for the Church's mission locally and globally, about roles, and notice which things seem to happen seamlessly. Talk about time, commitment, what people might offer inside and outside the church – in community situations and at worship.

- Ask each person to ask themselves what's next for them.

- Make a promise, plan a project, make connections that involve taking a risk.

- Maybe a project in the community – beer and hymns in the Red Lion? Whatever it is, it's their promise and nobody else's. It needs to be achievable and time-bound so that each person has a sense of achievement rather than failure.

I decided that I would give out the hymn books for ten weeks to all the children.

(Hannah, aged ten)

Taking leave of one another

Through this process – the fun, laughter, failure and simple experiential learning – God has created a flourishing community in this place. People have been empowered to move on, to belong and to take on roles and responsibilities they might not have considered previously.

Ask each of your group to give you a sentence to sum it all up – the message has been and continues to be that God loves the real you.

He sent Jesus to make that known through being present to us all.
He invites you to be loved and in time to respond more and more.

Finally, what will you do with your sentence – how will you offer it to the church community and get a response?

Prayer

This should be as arranged in the preparation, ending with a word of encouragement and blessing from your priest or representative of the church community.

Leaders' final reflection

Finally leaders, give thanks, take time to breathe out together. Have an evening out, evaluate what you've achieved – and forgive yourselves for what you have not achieved. You will know each other really well by now, so thank God for your incredible journey too.

11 Reviewing the Course

If we truly believed that Christ is the center of our life and world, that each of us is a member of the Body of Christ, and that body is incomplete without us, that the fullness of Christ encompasses all peoples . . . would we harm our neighbor? Injure or abuse the earth? Only in union with Christ, the One, can a person be united to the many since, as Word and Center of the Trinity, Christ is both the One and the Many.

(Ilea Delio)

A course evaluation example

Please note that, as would always be the case, this is an evaluation from a very particular situation and the scale and circumstances will always be factors to take into account. Small congregations might consider working together on producing a course.

The course of the parish in question has just completed its fourth year and the outcome of the leaders' self-evaluation is presented under four headings: people; sessions; future possibilities; what reduced or increased energy?

People

- The particular contribution made by lay leaders was in encouraging the group as companions on a journey.
- Although there's no need for clergy to be present at every session, selective involvement uses their expertise, links the group very clearly to the whole church and allows clergy to understand and respect the process.
- The format of the sessions allows people to learn in a 'simple' way.
- It was noted that the church and the leaders need to be clear regarding the purpose of the course. Is the aim to grow Christian community and individuals in their sense of being 'in Christ' and as 'God's people' in the whole of life? Is it a preparation for Confirmation? Or is it a mixed economy?
- There was a concern about excessive numbers. If there are more than ten travellers intimacy is lost.
- It's ideal to have two leaders so that group members have more than one role model. However, if there are more leaders it can be overwhelming if they're all present at every session.

- The course works best with a mixture of ages. Children present can keep everyone talking simply and more able to show vulnerability.

Sessions

- The suggested pattern of meetings 'in' and 'out' of church premises has seemed well balanced.
- If numbers of people are high, occasionally splitting into two groups has allowed more involvement by individuals.
- It's been important to follow the format agreed in the planning and not go off at a tangent. However, dealing with real issues that people raise, within careful time boundaries, gives weight to the statement that everyone's contribution counts.
- When for some reason a session didn't work out well, reviewing why that happened, and learning so that the leaders could move on, proved an effective approach.
- On this occasion it was noted that the effective elements within sessions were: sharing food, wine-making as a way of learning more about participation in the body and blood of Christ, music shared as a communication with a personal God and expressing joy, various ways of praying, exploring the church building and its 'secret' places, coming to know better the seasons of the Church's year, a visit to a cathedral, synagogue, Holy Island, and experiencing healing through laying on of hands with prayer.

Future possibilities

- Suppose we were to train an ecumenical group to take the course into their own churches.
- How about developing this to be focused around skills and interests of participants and leaders, for example art, computers, craft or gardening.
- Consider whom to invite as a new leader who would bring fresh ideas and energy. Allow if possible for an overlap of leaders from one course to the next to maximize the learning, building up of expertise and stability.

What reduced or increased energy?

Planning far enough ahead appeared to be a drain on energy and confidence. Suggestions to alleviate this included:

- Before the course begins, arrange the dates of all meetings, both in church and visits elsewhere.
- As the course begins, double-check on dates and visits.
- Resist rushing the course. It could run over several months, perhaps having

groups of meetings rather than weekly. A residential weekend may seem a luxury, but consider the value of running several sessions in two days and eating and spending some leisure time together.

- Although it seemed a good idea to plan the Confirmation two-thirds of the way through the course, in practice it didn't work out well.

- Progress and planning meetings for leaders worked well regarding communication and roles, but they would have been more manageable for busy people had they been more focused within an hour.

- Administrative work for a Confirmation can be quite complex. Allow time for this at an early stage.

- Sensitive leaders will vary in their energy levels, physically and emotionally. Take a good break between ending a course and starting to plan the next.

References and Further Reading

A New Zealand Prayer Book (1997), San Francisco: HarperSan Francisco, p. 181.

Alderman, Naomi, from *Disobedience*, quoted in Radcliffe, Timothy (2008), *Why Go to Church? The Drama of the Eucharist*, London: Continuum, p. 71.

Alexander, Irene (2007), *Dancing with God: Transformation through Relationship*, London: SPCK, p. 39.

Astley, Neil and Robertson-Pearce, Pamela (eds) (2007), *Soul Food: Nourishing Poems for Starving Minds*, Tarset: Bloodaxe.

Au, Wilkie (1990), *By Way of the Heart: Towards a Holistic Christian Spirituality*, London: Geoffrey Chapman, p. 155.

Bell, John L., quoted in Galloway, Kathy (2008), *Sharing the Blessing: Overcoming Poverty and Working for Justice*, London: SPCK, p. 46.

Billy, Dennis Joseph (1998), *Soliloquy Prayer: Unfolding our Hearts to God*, Chawton: Redemptorist Publications.

Billy, Dennis Joseph (1999), *Into the Heart of Faith: Ten Steps on the Journey*, Liguori, Mo.: Liguori Publications, p. 52.

Brown, Juanita and Isaacs, David (2005), *The World Café: Shaping our Futures through Conversations that Matter*, San Francisco: Berrett-Koehler.

Burgess, Ruth (2008), *Barefeet and Buttercups: Resources for Ordinary Time*, Glasgow: Wild Goose Publications.

Cooke, Bernard, in Borgeson, Josephine (ed.) (1990), *Reshaping Ministry: Essays in Memory of Wesley Frensdorff*, Arvada, Colo.: Jethro Publications, p. 19.

Cottrell, Stephen (2009), *The Things He Said*, London: SPCK, pp. 33, 57.

Delio, Ilea (2004), *Franciscan Prayer*, Cincinnati, Ohio: St Anthony Messenger Press, pp. 154–5.

Dix, Gregory, in Forrester, *Living and Loving the Mystery*, p. 90.

Donovan, Vincent J. (1978, 1982, 2001), *Christianity Rediscovered: An Epistle from the Masai*, Norwich: SCM Press, p. vii.

Dunn, James, quoted in Pickard, Stephen (2009), *Theological Foundations for Collaborative Ministry: Explorations in Practical, Pastoral and Empirical Theology*, Farnham: Ashgate, p. 37.

Endean, Philip, Foreword in *The Way* 44/3, p. 7.

Ford, David F. (1999), *Self and Salvation: Being Transformed*, Cambridge: Cambridge University Press, p. 133.

Forrester, Duncan B. (2001), *On Human Worth*, Norwich: SCM Press, p. 199.

Forrester, Duncan B. (2010), *Living and Loving the Mystery: Exploring Christian Worship*, Edinburgh: St Andrew Press, pp. 9, 38, 84.

Furnon, Jean-Marc (2009), 'The Mass that Takes its Time', *The Way* 48/1, p. 63.

Godly Play: see <www.godlyplay.org.uk>.

Greenwood, Robin (2009), *Parish Priests: For the Sake of the Kingdom*, London: SPCK.

Hardy, Daniel W. (2010), *Wording a Radiance: Parting Conversations on God and the Church*, Norwich: SCM Press, p. 65.

Jackson, Gordon, quoted in Lartey, Emmanuel Y. (2006), *Pastoral Theology in an Intercultural World*, Peterborough: Epworth, p. 22.

Jenson, Matt and Wilhite, David (2010), *The Church: A Guide for the Perplexed*, London, T&T Clark.

Hauerwas, Stanley (2004), *Performing the Faith: Bonhoeffer and the Practice of Nonviolence*, London: SPCK, p. 14.

Houston, Gaie (1990), *The Red Book of Groups and How to Lead Them Better*, London: Rochester Foundation.

Kanyoro, Musimbi, 'The Shape of God to Come and the Future of Humanity', *Concilium*, 2004/5, pp. 53ff.

Keller, Catherine, quoted in Grey, Mary C., 2000, *The Outrageous Pursuit of Hope: Prophetic Dreams for the Twenty-First Century*, London: Darton, Longman & Todd, p. 7.

King, Nicholas (2005), 'The New Testament as Holy Ground', *The Way* 44/2, p. 68.

Kirkpatrick, Damian, Doherty, Philip and O'Flynn, Sheelagh (eds) (2002), *Joy in All Things: A Franciscan Companion*, Norwich: Canterbury Press, p. 90.

Lavin, Margaret (2004), *Theology for Ministry*, Ottawa: Novalis, pp. 116, 126.

Lawrence, Louise J. (2009), *The Word in Place: Reading the New Testament in Contemporary Contexts*, London: SPCK, p. 154.

McAlpin, Kathleen (2009), *Ministry That Transforms: A Contemplative Process of Theological Reflection*, Collegeville, Minn.: Liturgical Press, pp. 1, 4, 10.

McFague, Sallie, in Lawrence, Louise J., *The Word in Place*, p. 132.

McMichael, Ralph (2010), *Eucharist: A Guide for the Perplexed*, London: T&T Clark.

Marty, François, 'Body and Memory in African Liturgy', *Concilium*, 1995/3, p. 26.

Mor Coorilos, Geevarghese, Plenary Speech at Edinburgh International Church Conference, 3 June 2010.

Muller, Peter and Fernandez de Aranguiz, Angel (2010), *Every Pilgrim's Guide to Walking to Santiago de Compostela*, trans. Laurie Dennett, Norwich: Canterbury Press.

O'Meara, Thomas, in McAlpin, Kathleen, *Ministry That Transforms*, p. 8.

Papandrea, James L. (2009), *Spiritual Blueprint: How We Live, Work, Love, Play and Pray*, Liguori, Mo.: Liguori Publications, p. ix.

Pears, Angie (2010), *Doing Contextual Theology*, London: Routledge, pp. 166f.

Pennington, Basil (1995), Foreword in Eberhard Arnold, *Why We Live in Community: With Two Interpretive Talks by Thomas Merton*, Robertsbridge/Farmington, Penn.: Plough Publishing House, pp. xiii–xiv.

Pritchard, John (1997), *The Intercessions Handbook*, London: SPCK, pp. 119–20.

Rachower, Jossel, quoted in Bassett, Lytta (2007), *Holy Anger: Jacob, Job, Jesus*, London: Continuum, pp. 94f.

Radcliffe, Timothy, quoted in Holyhead, Verna A. (2006), *With Burning Hearts: Welcoming the Word in Year C*, Collegeville, Minn.: Liturgical Press, p. 105

Radcliffe, Timothy (2008), *Why Go to Church? The Drama of the Eucharist*, London: Continuum, pp. 68, 100.

Rendle, Gil and Mann, Alice (2003), *Holy Conversations: Strategic Planning as a Spiritual Practice for Congregations*, Bethesda, Md.: The Alban Institute, p. 49.

Rohr, Richard (2008), *Things Hidden: Scripture as Spirituality*, Cincinnati, Ohio: St Anthony Messenger Press, pp. 54, 61, 215.

Rohr, Richard (2009), *The Naked Now: Learning to See as the Mystics See*, New York: Crossroad, pp. 95f.

Romero, Oscar, quoted in Ashley, J. Matthew (2005) 'Oscar Romero, Religion and Spirituality', *The Way* 44/2, p. 123.

Scharmer, C. Otto (2009), *Theory U: Leading from the Future as it Emerges: The Social Technology of Presencing*, San Francisco: Berrett-Koehler, p. xvi.

Schüssler Fiorenza, Elisabeth, in McAlpin, Kathleen, *Ministry That Transforms*, p. 93.

Shea, John (2010), *Following Jesus*, New York: Orbis, pp. 81, 126.

Thew Forrester, Kevin L. (2003), *I Have Called You Friends*, New York: Church Publishing, pp. 8, 101.

Thurston, Bonnie (2005), 'Words and the Word: Reflections on Scripture, Prayer and Poetry', *The Way* 44/2, p. 20.

Thurston, Bonnie (2009), 'On Biblical Preaching', *The Way* 48/1, p. 68.

Tutu, Desmond, quoted in Janet Hodgson (2010), *Making the Sign of the Cross: A Creative Resource for Seasonal Worship, Retreats and Quiet Days*, Norwich: Canterbury Press, p. 2.

Volf, Miroslav (1996), *Exclusion and Embrace: A Theological Exploration of Identity, Otherness, and Reconciliation*, Nashville, Tenn.: Abingdon Press, p. 129.

Walton, Martin (1995), *Marginal Communities: The Ethical Enterprise of the Followers of Jesus*, Kampen: Kok Pharos, p. 253.

Ward, Graham (2009), *The Politics of Discipleship: Becoming Postmaterial Citizens*, Grand Rapids, Mich.: Baker Academic, pp. 181–2.

Wells, Samuel (2006), *God's Companions: Reimagining Christian Ethics*, Oxford: Blackwell, p. 2.

Whitworth, Patrick (2008), *Prepare for Exile: A New Spirituality and Mission for the Church*, London: SPCK, p. 98.

Williams, Rowan (2004), *Anglican Identities*, London: Darton, Longman & Todd, pp. 7, 96.

World Council of Churches (1982), *Baptism, Eucharist and Ministry*, Geneva: WCC.